£20.00

Teaching and Learning Early Years Mathematics

Subject and Pedagogic Knowledge

CRITICAL
TEACHING

You might also like the following books in our *Critical Teaching* series

Beyond Early Reading
Edited by David Waugh and Sally Neaum
978-1-909330-41-2 September 2013

Primary School Placements: A Critical Guide to Outstanding Teaching
By Catriona Robinson, Branwen Bingle and Colin Howard
978-1-909330-45-0 In print

Teaching Systematic Synthetic Phonics and Early English
By Jonathan Glazzard and Jane Stokoe
978-1-909330-09-2 In print

Most of our titles are also available in a range of electronic formats. To order please
to our website www.criticalpublishing.com or contact our distributor, NBN Internatio
10 Thornbury Road, Plymouth PL6 7PP, telephone 01752 202301 or email orde
nbninternational.com.

Teaching and Learning Early Years Mathematics

Subject and Pedagogic Knowledge

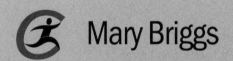 Mary Briggs

CRITICAL
TEACHING

First published in 2013 by Critical Publishing Ltd

British Library Cataloguing in Publication Data
A CIP record for this book is available from the British Library

ISBN: 978-1-909330-37-5

This book is also available in the following e-book formats:

Kindle ISBN: 978-1-909330-38-2
EPUB ISBN: 978-1-909330-39-9
Adobe e-book ISBN: 978-1-909330-40-5

Cover design by Greensplash Limited
Project Management by Out of House Publishing
Printed and bound in Great Britain by T J International Ltd.

Critical Publishing
152 Chester Road
Northwich
CW8 4AL
www.criticalpublishing.com

Contents

Meet the author

Mary Briggs is an Associate Professor at the Institute of Education, University of Warwick. Mary has taught in a range of special and mainstream schools. She is currently a teacher and researcher on education programmes from undergraduate to doctoral level at the University. She has acted as a consultant on the learning and teaching of mathematics for a number of organisations. Mary has written extensively about mathematics education across the early years and primary age range and passionately believes that everyone can understand and enjoy mathematics and that it can be taught in interesting and creative ways.

1 Introduction

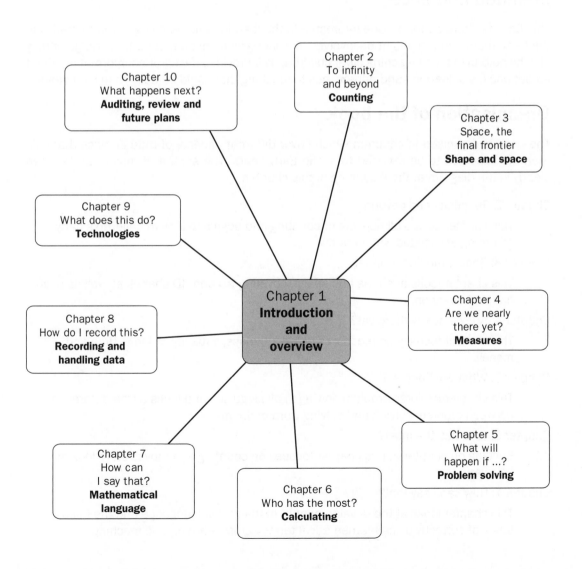

Introduction

Welcome to this book about the learning and teaching of mathematics in the early years. This chapter gives an overview of the whole book and discusses how the book might be used, by whom and when. It also describes the key features of this book and how these can be explored.

Aim of the book

The aim of this book is to explore subject knowledge alongside pedagogic ideas about the learning and teaching of mathematics in the early years, spanning the current Foundation Stage and the start of primary schooling in Key Stage 1, that is, children from three- to eight-years old. It can be read from cover to cover, although readers may find it useful to dip in and out depending on what aspect of mathematics they are concentrating on within their practice.

Intended audience

This book is intended for anyone interested in the learning and teaching of mathematics in the Early Years and who might be involved in working with children in that age range. It may also be helpful to those teaching older children, as it provides background information about earlier phases of learning and approaches to teaching that could be built on in later years.

Organisation of the book

The book is organised in chapters which cover different aspects of mathematics that children are expected to be exposed to in the Early Years. The spread of topics can be seen clearly in the diagram at the beginning of this chapter.

Chapter 2: To infinity and beyond

> This chapter covers all aspects of counting and begins to look at children's early recording associated with quantity.

Chapter 3: Space, the final frontier

> This chapter looks at shape and space, covering 2D and 3D shapes as well as position and direction.

Chapter 4: Are we nearly there yet?

> This chapter focuses on measures of length, mass, capacity, volume, time and money.

Chapter 5: What will happen if...?

> This chapter explores problem solving in all its guises and looks at the difference between problem solving and solving word problems.

Chapter 6: Who has the most?

> Building on chapter 2, this chapter focuses on counting and moves on to look at calculating.

Chapter 7: How can I say that?

> This chapter looks at the development of mathematical language and the importance of correctly using mathematical terms across learning and teaching.

Chapter 8: How do I record this?

This chapter explores the move from mark making towards formal recording; it also looks at the wide range of ways in which young children can record their ideas for themselves and others.

Chapter 9: What does this do?

This chapter discusses the use of different technologies to support the learning and teaching of mathematics.

Chapter 10: What happens next?

The final chapter offers an opportunity for the reader to reflect upon what they have learnt from this book, to audit their subject knowledge and the provision in their setting/school, and to create an action plan for continuing professional development that may be individually or organisationally focused.

Answers

This section provides answers to most of the *Test your subject knowledge* questions that appear throughout the book.

Glossary

This section unpacks some of the key terms used in the book and gives definitions to support understanding and subject knowledge.

Structure of each chapter

Each chapter starts with an introductory diagram that shows the connections within the chapter, providing an at-a-glance overview of the main themes of the chapter content. We discuss children's initial, often innate, understanding of the aspect where appropriate, and point out possible sources of misconceptions.

Key features of each chapter

Each key feature is meant to offer a starting point for the reader, rather than to suggest an exhaustive list of all possible options. Most of the features are designed to stimulate readers' creativity, so that they can adapt and explore other similar opportunities for learning and teaching mathematics in their own practice.

Focus on research

This feature focuses on relevant research associated with the areas of mathematics explored in the chapter and asks critical questions about the implications for practice.

International perspectives

This feature looks at research and practises in context in other countries around the world.

Critical questions

These questions are designed to make the reader think more deeply about the issues being discussed. Sometimes they relate to subject knowledge and sometimes to practice. After most critical questions there are comments that pick up the themes which might have been considered in response to the question(s) asked. These comments are also intended to act as triggers for asking further questions concerning research and practice, even when the text doesn't suggest them, so that practitioners will develop an attitude of critical analysis rather than simple acceptance of what has been presented. Might there be alternative perspectives on the same issue? What would be the impact of viewing this issue in a different way?

Specific adult-led activities to encourage and develop children's mathematical skills

This feature suggests a range of activities to be guided by adults for small groups of children, in order to explore the key ideas relating to the aspects of mathematics covered in each chapter. If several different aspects are explored in a chapter, there may be more than one list of suggested activities.

Sigel (2002) suggests that the goal of cognitive socialisation is to *generate reconstituted schemas that have the potential for being expressed in the appropriate symbolic mode* (Sigel, 2002, page 190). Adult-led activities are designed to assist children in making the connections that allow them to move towards the abstraction and symbolism required in later learning of mathematics and which they will not make solely through their own exploration of the environment. This aspect can be challenging for many adults working in early years education, as they might have concerns about their own subject knowledge and confidence with mathematics. The adult-led activities are typically short activities which can be undertaken indoors or outdoors to encourage children to focus specifically on the aspect of mathematics under discussion.

Activities as part of continuous provision

In addition to specifically planned activities, there should be resources available in locations around the setting from which the children can choose. Such continuous provision in the setting enables children to explore aspects of mathematics learning throughout the day. These opportunities can be table-top activities for sorting or counting, or they could include games for children to choose. The activities should be changed regularly to offer children a range of stimuli for their mathematical learning, and should always include both indoor and outdoor opportunities.

The following table shows an example overview of the selection of activities linked to the current curriculum area including mathematics, with a focus on resources, vocabulary and adult input where appropriate.

Specific activity or area, eg, sand and water		
Key learning objectives linked to the current curriculum		Resources to include
		Vocabulary
Adult input		

Play environments

These are areas of the setting/school that are developed in collaboration with the children, to help them explore mathematical ideas, language and recording. The description of each play environment is organised under the following headings.

Idea: the overarching theme of the environment to be created.

Equipment: suggestions of equipment that could be used to establish the specific thematic area.

Outcomes: some possible outcomes of the play, often described in terms of observable behaviours.

Assessing children's skills

This list is intended to give the reader some initial ideas for the kinds of assessment related to the theme of each chapter. These are the key areas for which evidence could be gathered to judge whether children can do, or demonstrate that they know, a certain aspect of mathematics.

Test your subject knowledge

This feature offers an opportunity for the reader to test their understanding of key terms or mathematical processes where appropriate. In some chapters, the 'Test your subject knowledge' and 'Extend your subject knowledge' features have been combined. Answers to most of the questions are given at the end of the book.

Extend your subject knowledge

This feature is aimed at the adult reader and suggests some aspects of the mathematics in each chapter that might be explored further to extend personal mathematical subject knowledge.

Critical learning points from this chapter

This section summarises the key aspects covered in the chapter.

Critical reflection

This section links the theory and ideas explored in the chapter to current practice and asks the reader to consider how they might integrate the ideas into their own practice through observation or review.

Taking it further

This is an annotated list of possible other publications to read, focusing on specific aspects explored in the chapter; these publications could include research articles, websites, or chapters of other books.

References

This is a list of references to all books or articles cited in the chapter, to enable the reader to follow up on specific materials that have been referred to in the text.

Taking it further

Ginsburg, H P and Amit, M (2008) What is Teaching Mathematics to Young Children? A Theoretical Perspective and Case Study. *Journal of Applied Developmental Psychology*, 29: 274–85.

This article looks critically at the issue of adult-led, as opposed to child-initiated, activities in mathematics and their impact on disadvantaged children's future learning of mathematics.

References

Sigel, I E (2002) The Psychological Distancing Model: A Study of the Socialization of Cognition. *Culture & Psychology*, 8(2): 189–214.

2 To infinity and beyond

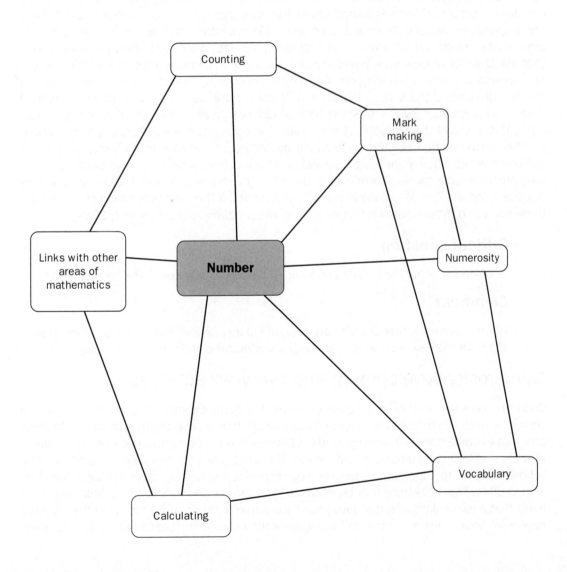

Counting

Mark making

Links with other areas of mathematics

Number

Numerosity

Calculating

Vocabulary

Introduction

This chapter looks at young children's acquisition of number, unpacks the essential subject knowledge you will need, and explores some ways to engage young children with this aspect of mathematics. Number is often seen as the dominant area of mathematics in any curriculum. You will need to understand how children develop their skills in counting, which then leads to calculating. You will also need to be aware of what children may already know before they attend nursery or school.

Starting to count

Children start to make sense of quantity very early. Researchers focusing on the brain, such as Brian Butterworth (1999), believe that babies are born with a kind of start-up kit for learning about numbers that is coded in the genome. Even in the first week of life, babies are sensitive to changes in the number of things that they are looking at, and at six months they can do very simple addition and subtraction. Psychologists such as Karen Wynn (1992) have investigated pre-verbal children and their ability to understand different quantities. Whether the children are actually counting is difficult to say, but they are paying attention to situations that are novel or unexpected. Wynn showed a baby a doll, covered the doll with a screen, and showed a second doll being placed behind the screen. The baby would then expect to see two dolls when the screen is removed. If there turns out to be a different number of dolls – either more or fewer – then the baby would look longer than if there were exactly two dolls. This is called the 'violation of expectation' experiment. Researchers studying infants' number-discrimination abilities have taken advantage of the fact that infants tend to be more interested when something they see is different from what they have seen before. If they are shown the same picture over and over again, they will look at it less and less. This decline in the amount of looking is called 'habituation'. If the infants are then shown something novel or different, renewed looking, or 'dishabituation', occurs (Frantz, 1964).

Critical question

»   *What do you think the babies are doing in Wynn's experiment? Are they counting?*

Comment

There is evidence that children are reacting to a situation that they are not expecting, although the research doesn't actually show that the children are counting.

Numerosity development and everyday activities

Children make sense of quantity early on without actually counting. For example, they can collect two nappies by knowing that they have enough if they have one in each hand. Children also make connections between quantities of things through being involved in everyday activities such as laying the table and making sure there is a place for everyone in the family. This is how they start to understand one-to-one correspondence, that is, the matching of one item with another. The other thing that children begin to see is specific patterns of numbers. They learn that a particular pattern always shows the same number, and as a result they can tell how many items there are in that pattern without actually counting each item. This is referred to as 'subitising'. Subitising occurs with patterns that are easy to recognise, such as the arrangements of dots that appear on dice.

Young children's experiences with oral counting

Young children start to count as part of learning nursery rhymes and songs. The counting can often be heard as an unbroken chain of sound with the individual items running together, eg, 'wuntoofreeforfive'. At the same time, children often learn the alphabet and recite it also as a chain where the components are not seen as individual letters. At this stage they are concentrating on the tune or sound of the process rather than the words of the song and the individual letters or numbers – these are not heard by the children as separate items. Breaking this chain is essential in learning to accurately count a group of items and, later on, for 'counting on' and answering questions like 'What is the number after...?' Children want to show others that they can count and are often heard to say things like 'I can count high'. However, learning to recite numbers in the correct order is not the same as knowing that when you count objects you can tell how many you have. This is a common assumption mistakenly made by adults; the two skills have to come together for children to be able to count effectively.

Abilities associated with memorisation of the number word sequence

There are a number of things associated with memorising the number sequence that children need to be able to do in order to count accurately. Children need to be able to recite:

- the sequence starting from one;
- the sequence starting from one and stopping at a given number word;
- the sequence starting at a given number word that is not necessarily one;
- the sequence starting at a given number word and stopping at another given number word;
- the sequence backwards from a given number word, eg, 10, 9, 8, 7, 6, 5, 4, 3, 2, 1, blast off is a favourite;
- the sequence backwards from a given number word and stopping at another given number word, eg, 8, 7, 6, 5, 4, 3, 2.

Difficulties with counting

Counting may seem very straightforward to an adult, but a variety of mistakes can occur, and adults working with young children need to listen very carefully, check for mistakes and gently correct them, so that children can continue to develop their counting skills. Counting mistakes can take the following forms.

- A word is omitted from the sequence – eg, one, two, four, five.

- Words are in the wrong order in the recited sequence (which, surprisingly, is a less common mistake but does occur) – eg, one, two, three, five, four, six.

- Words are repeated in the sequence – eg, one, two, three, three, four.

- Recitation of the sequence does not start from the beginning (ie, one); this is an opportunity for the teacher to make clear to children the purpose of the activity – eg, 'If I want to know how many I need, then I must start at one unless I am counting on.'

- The teen words are particularly tricky and mistakes can be made by analogy – eg, thirteen, fourteen, fiveteen, or twenty-nine, twenty-ten.

Mistakes other than with recitation

There are a number of other issues with counting that can cause children problems and lead to inaccurate counting.

- Co-ordination can be an issue, as children might 'skim' over items or create 'flurry' errors by moving their hands too quickly over the set of items to be counted.

- Children may have problems keeping track of where they started with counting a number of items; this can result in items being counted twice or ignored.

- Children may have difficulties deciding in which order to count items, especially if the items are not arranged in a line or other obvious pattern.

Keeping track of counting

Children keep track in one of three ways when they start to count.

1. Visual counters 'point' with their eyes or head movements but do not actually touch the items to be counted.

2. Touch counters touch each item to be counted.

3. Physical partitioners move items as they count to ensure that they have counted each item in turn.

Children often need the security of one or more of these methods of keeping track, and there are no problems with using any of these methods as long as they work and result in accurate counting for the child.

Accurate counting and the key principles

In order to be able to count accurately, children need to be able to give each item being counted an individual label, ie, one number name for each item. The number name list must be used in the same fixed order on each occasion; counters must not change the order of the number names that they use to count. The order in which the items are counted does not matter, however, as long as the child doing the counting can keep track of where they started and where they will finish, ensuring that they count each item only once. The last number name used gives the number of objects in the set. The arrangement of the items to be counted does not make any difference to the total number in the set. These points can be summarised as the following principles of counting.

Five principles of counting skills

The first three principles are about how to count, and the last two are about what can be counted (Gelman and Gellistel, 1978).

1. *One-to-one principle* – there is one and only one distinct counting word for each object.

2. *Stable order principle* – the number words and their order are unique.

3. *Cardinal principle* – the last name used in the count has a special status; it tells the counter how many items are in the set.

4. *No restriction or abstraction principle* – there is no restriction on the collections of items that can be counted, and these can be real or imaginary.

5. *Object order irrelevant principle* – the order in which the items are counted does not matter, although the order of the number words does.

Children find the 'object order irrelevant principle' difficult to grasp until counting has become an embedded skill. For children to be able to count easily, their recitation of the number sequence must be as a fluid numerable chain of number names. Piaget argued that children cannot be considered 'counters' if they could not 'conserve' number. His test of conservation is a well-tried task in which children are asked if there are more counters in one row than the other, or if the two rows have the same number of counters.

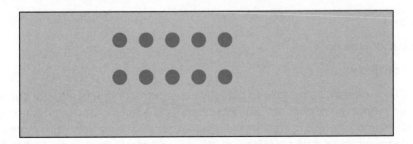

Children readily agree that there is the same number of counters in each row. The next step in the task is for the adult to spread out one row of counters as shown on the following page while the child is watching.

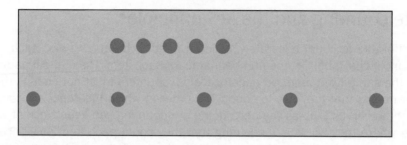

The adult then asks the child the same question as before. The new visual image of the situation may change young children's thinking, and they might say that the spread-out row has more counters as it appears to be longer. These children, Piaget would say, cannot conserve number and so should not be seen as counters.

Critical question

» *How far do you agree with Piaget that children cannot be considered 'counters' if they cannot conserve number under the conditions of his test?*

Comment

Although the Piagetian test is reliable and repeatable, there have been many criticisms of the test. Ginsburg tried a version of the task using two jars of counters where the children were not able to see the counters being moved, although they could see the counters that were going into each jar. The children were able to tell if one jar had more or fewer counters inside than the other. Since they were not influenced by the visual image, this demonstrated their understanding of comparisons of quantities and their ability to identify more or less. From the results of this experiment you may feel that children can be seen as 'counters' without 'passing' the Piagetian test.

The purpose of counting

As they begin to develop their counting skills, very young children find the idea of a purpose for counting difficult. Penny Munn (1994) explored this issue with pre-school children and found that the children identified three purposes of counting. In order of priority, these are:

1. for play;

2. as a performance;

3. to reveal quantity.

Munn found that, despite being able to actually carry out counting tasks well before starting school, a high proportion of children did not understand adults' purposes (Munn, 1997). The children's ideas about counting came from social experiences, so they were more concerned about the pleasures of counting or pleasing others, and rarely linked counting to finding out 'how many'. What Munn also found was that activities given to children in pre-school settings emphasised counting skills but did not include discussion of the purpose behind the task. Munn continued to refine her 'purpose of counting' categories into four, which summarise the ideas above. Children count:

1. to please themselves;

2. to conform to others' expectations;

3. in order to learn;

4. to know how many there are.

It is your role as a teacher to ensure that children understand the purpose of counting activities so that they can make the link between what they are doing and ideas about counting.

Difficulties that might occur

The following, taken from Ginsburg's research, are some of the problems that might occur around counting.

1. The ability to say the numbers does not guarantee their effective application.

2. The accurate use of words does not guarantee understanding.

3. To develop effective counting skills, young children require repetitive experience in counting things and can get this in virtually any environment.

4. Young children are engaged in the spontaneous learning of economical strategies for counting things.

5. Young children must relearn with larger numbers what they already know about smaller ones.

(Ginsburg, 1977, pages 20 and 29)

Some of these issues, such as the first two points in the list, arise from assumptions that adults make about children's abilities based on performance rather than understanding. The third point in the list concerns the adult's role in providing opportunities for children to practise skills. The fourth point is linked to the idea of 'subitising', ie, spotting a pattern and not needing to count each item individually; it could also mean that children spontaneously begin to count larger numbers in twos. The final point Ginsburg makes may sound strange, but the structure of English counting means that children essentially relearn the counting number names between 11 and 20, as these don't initially appear to follow a clear pattern. After 20, the orderly pattern of number names (the tens plus a unit) emerges.

Extending counting

Once you have established that children can count in one direction, accurately assigning one label (number name) to each item counted, you know that they have acquired the knowledge of the numerable chain. You can then move on to develop their ability to count from a number other than 1; for example, children can practise counting up from 6 to 9. You can also help them understand the idea of the bi-directional chain, ie, that counting words can be produced fluently in either direction – they can count up or down the number sequence (Fuson, 1988).

INTERNATIONAL PERSPECTIVE

Counting and calculating frames

In Norway children are initially introduced to a counting frame with only five spaces.

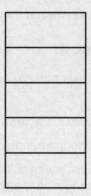

Items are placed in the frame and children asked about what they can see.

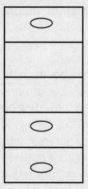

One child might say that they can see three items in the frame, while another would notice the two spaces without items. This not only helps children with counting individual items but also emphasises the relationship between the numbers involved; in this example, the number of items and the number of spaces give the relationship 3 + 2 = 5, or 5 − 2 = 3. At no point are children in Norway asked to write these calculations down; nor do the adults record these for the children. The discussion of the situation is the key to developing understanding.

Items can be placed on the frame in different ways, so the frame can be used again and again to stimulate discussion. Frames can also be given to children for them to explore on their own – for example, a frame which is a series of identical boxes fixed together, a frame drawn on paper, or a frame constructed on a large scale outdoors.

Once children are comfortable with a five-space frame, they are introduced to one with ten spaces.

Malleable boards for modelling number bonds to ten

In the UK, the emphasis has been more on checking that the children know specific facts rather than on exploration and discussion, which is the focus in Norway. Children in the UK are encouraged to show their knowledge through the use of equipment such as the malleable boards illustrated below. These are patterns of usually ten items that can be folded to show specific numbers.

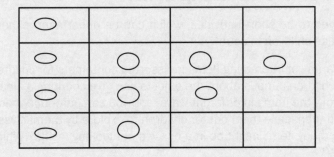

These boards can be made from paper or card, scored and laminated so that they fold easily. The idea is that each child has a board and when they are asked, for example, to 'show me four', they can then be asked, 'How many do you see?' The children should be able to see six, with four and six making the total of ten items on the board. The items on the boards could be personalised to match each child's interests (eg, cars, dolls), and children could make their own by selecting or drawing an object which is then photocopied to give ten of the same.

Critical question

» *Consider the differences in approach to developing children's counting skills in Norway and the UK. What kinds of models do you have available for children to encourage attention to number bonds in your class or setting?*

Comment

The two approaches, though different, both offer models for children to use in developing their understanding of numbers and number bonds to ten. You may have identified other models that you make available for children. If such models are not currently available in your setting, they would be worth trying, as they offer children the opportunity to actively engage with number and get familiar with number bonds.

What to notice when children are playing

Part of the skill of working with children mathematically is to observe and listen carefully to what they say. You may hear private speech that is not really intended for others or thoughts articulated out loud. You may hear children using counting words in their activities. You should also pay attention to behaviours which indicate that children are using counting knowledge in their play – for example, setting the table for the three bears, sharing out sweets among dolls, or counting the bricks needed to make a wall. Watch out for children matching one item to another, such as cars to garages. Only by listening and observing can you identify the knowledge children already have and determine the most appropriate intervention to take their learning further.

Specific adult-led activities to encourage and develop children's counting skills

These are designed to be short activities, which can be undertaken either indoors or outdoors, to encourage children to count.

* Collect a variety of interesting items in assorted containers for children to count. This will make children curious about the objects and give counting a clear purpose. It helps to store the items in different ways, and you can introduce them in a specific activity and then leave them out for children to explore by themselves. Can children guess how many items might be in a box without looking inside? Which box holds the most items?

* Place numbers in various locations outdoors for children to find, collect and then order correctly.

* Try activities that involve the children clapping a specific number of times. Alternatively, you could ask one child to do a certain activity, such as hopping on one leg, for a specified number of times while the rest of the group counts; or you could get everyone doing the activity at the same time.

* Read stories that involve counting items and collecting them together – for example, *The Shopping Basket* (Burningham, 1992). As the story is read, the items are collected by different children and placed in a basket.

* Roll a dice, collect that number of items and place them into a basket or box. This can be done by each child or by the group as a whole.

* Giant board games such as snakes and ladders can provide good practice for counting. As the dice is rolled, children acting as counters walk on the correct number of spaces.

- Nursery rhymes and stories involving counting can stimulate discussions about counting and its purposes.

- How many items can children fit into a small box? (Make sure the children all have boxes of the same size.) Who has the most items? Who has the fewest? Which children have the same number of items?

- Challenge children to collect a specific number of items, and give them a countdown to complete the task.

- Ask children to collect a specific number of items to make a shape – for example, four straws to make a square or oblong. This helps children make the connection between counting and the properties of different shapes.

Activities as part of continuous provision

In addition to specifically planned activities, there should be resources available in locations around the setting from which the children can choose, enabling them to explore various aspects of counting. These could include:

- stairs that are numbered to help children count up and down the steps;

- number lines and number tracks outdoors and indoors;

- number books in English and other languages;

- large beads on string for counting;

- number labelling of any appropriate sets of objects or locations, such as aprons on hooks or bays for bikes;

- collections of interesting things in containers for children to explore, sort and count.

Play environments for children to explore counting

Different kinds of play environments provide children with opportunities to explore specific aspects of mathematics as well as to use mathematical language appropriately and reinforce their skills. Although initially you may set up an area for children to explore, it is important that they be able to add to and develop the environment as they play, changing the emphasis according to their needs and interests. The following ideas are meant to provide starting points for creating your own play environments.

Button shop or badge shop

Idea

Set up a shop with items that can easily be sorted and counted.

Equipment

Button cards or lots of badges for sorting and counting.

Outcomes

Children identify patterns of buttons that they recognise and hence don't need to count. They can count other items and make larger and smaller sets of buttons or badges.

Fishing pool

Idea

Children are encouraged to fish for numbers or items which they can then sort, count, compare and/or put in order.

Equipment

Nets and fishing rods; numbers or fish, depending upon the focus of the activity; buckets for the catch; aprons or protective clothing to prevent children from getting too wet.

Outcomes

Children will count their catch after each game and compare their catch with others' using vocabulary such as 'more', 'less' and 'the same'. This could involve the children counting items, comparing sets of items, ordering the numbers collected, and determining which number(s) they might be missing in a given sequence.

Velcro wall

Idea

Children stick velcro items onto a material-backed wall and count the items, or numbers are stuck onto the wall which children can order and count.

Equipment

Felt or similar material attached to a low wall, either indoors or outdoors where it is protected from wet weather; items with velcro attached to them so that they can be placed on the wall.

Outcomes

Children can create their own patterns of items for counting and practise ordering numerals. This can be a good activity for assessing children's knowledge while observing them at play.

Number corner

Idea

Set aside a specific area, such as one corner of the room, for a particular number, so that everything in that area is in sets of the given number. For example, if the chosen number is 3, everything in the corner must be in threes, although there may be several different kinds of items.

Equipment

A variety of objects in sets of a given number; for example, if 3 is the given number, you might have three aprons, three masks, three chairs, three cushions, and so on.

Outcomes

In the case of 3 being the given number, this activity would give children the feel of the 'three-ness' of 3 in various forms, emphasising that the number 3 is the same for different sets of objects, some big and some small. This may encourage children to find their own sets of three to add to the corner.

Assessing children's counting skills

*   How far can the child count orally?

*   How many objects can the child reliably count?

*   Can the child count backwards?

*   Can the child count sets of different kinds of items?

*   Can the child count on from a given number and stop at another given number, eg, count on from 6 and stop at 10?

*   Can the child answer questions like 'What number comes before 8 when counting?' or 'What number comes before 5?'

*   Can the child make a specific item in a set number 6 (understand the object order irrelevance principle)?

Test your subject knowledge

Counting is often seen as a simple activity that small children can do, but that is if we focus on small whole positive numbers. There are different ways, or patterns, of counting; for example, counting in twos gives the same results as the two times table.

1.   In each of the following counting patterns, there are some missing numbers. Can you complete the counting in each case?

(a)   ___, ___, ___, 39, ___, 59, ___, 79

(b)   ___, 896, ___, ___, 905, 908, ___, ___,

(c)   −15, −10, −5, ___, ___, ___, ___,

(d)   8, 28, ___, ___, ___, ___, ___, ___, ___, 188

2.   Is an integer a rational number?

3.   Is π a rational or an irrational number?

Extend your subject knowledge

There is a tendency to consider counting as something we do with just whole positive numbers, ie, 1, 2, 3 and so on. However, there are other sets of numbers besides the positive whole numbers.

Types of numbers

»   *Natural or counting numbers*

These are the positive whole numbers we encounter all the time; they do not include zero.

»   *Whole numbers*

These are like the natural numbers but with zero added to the set, ie, 0, 1, 2, 3,...

»   *Integers*

These are all the whole numbers between positive infinity and negative infinity:

$$..., -6, -5, -4, -3, -2, -1, 0, 1, 2, 3, 4, 5, 6,...$$

»   *Rational numbers*

A rational number is a number that can be expressed as a fraction or ratio; some examples are:

$$\tfrac{6}{1} \text{ or } 6 \text{ or } 6.0, -2 \text{ or } -\tfrac{2}{1} \text{ or } -2.0, \tfrac{1}{2} \text{ or } 0.5$$

»   *Irrational numbers*

Irrational numbers cannot be expressed as fractions; an example is $\sqrt{2}$.

Moving from counting to calculating

As children move from counting to calculating, they use the skills they have been developing with counting to assist them in calculating orally with small numbers.

Carpenter and Moser (1984) proposed a set of strategies that children use to calculate addition problems.

•   *Count all.* This is a strategy whereby, if a child has two different quantities of objects, say 3 and 5, each set of items is first counted separately so that the child has a set of 3 and a set of 5; the child then combines the two sets and counts all of the items again, to obtain 8. This is a laborious process with several stages, and therefore contains multiple opportunities for errors to occur.

- *Count on from the first number.* This is a strategy that children often use naturally without being shown how, and it shortens the process from counting all. In this case, children recognise the number of items in one set and then continue counting the items in the second set to find how many there are in total. For example, a child might recognise the pattern of items as meaning there are three in one set, and then count on from four in the second set: 4, 5, 6, 7, 8.

- *Count on from the larger number.* This strategy shortens the previous one again and leads to greater efficiency. If the child starts with recognising the larger number and counts on from it, they will have less remaining to count. For example, with a set of three objects and a set of five objects, the child recognises the larger set as containing five and then counts 6, 7, 8.

- *Use a known number fact.* There is no counting involved in this strategy. The child uses existing knowledge of a fact to recall the answer to a calculation. The known facts often start with doubles, such as 2 + 2 = 4, 3 + 3 = 6, 4 + 4 = 8, 5 + 5 = 10 and so on.

- *Use a known fact to derive another fact.* In this strategy, the child uses a known fact to help them work out another fact. This strategy moves further away from direct counting. For example, if the child already knows that 4 + 4 = 8, they can work out that 4 + 5 = 9.

Assessing children's early calculating skills

Can the child:

- accurately count all of the items in a set;
- use counting to identify the larger of two sets of items;
- do simple addition by counting on from one number;
- do simple addition by counting on from the larger number;
- tell you some known facts about adding numbers (they are likely to start with doubles such as 2 + 2 = 4);
- derive a fact from a known fact?

Specific adult-led activities to encourage and develop children's calculating skills

- Throw two dice and ask children to add the two numbers together. This is a good starting point for leading children into calculating.

- For this activity you will need a box to be a bus, a set of toys to act as passengers, and a number of bus stops around a circle. Children can put in or take off passengers at each bus stop, and the number of passengers on the bus can then be calculated; this allows children to explore the relationships between the number of people on the bus, the number waiting at a bus stop, and the number who get off at the stop. For example, if three people are currently on the bus, and there are two waiting at the next bus stop, how many passengers will the bus have after the next stop? Similar calculations can be done with passengers getting off at the next stop.

FOCUS ON RESEARCH

Mark making

While developing number sense, children begin to record their own ideas about quantity. A number of researchers have investigated how children's mark making might be categorised. The first was Martin Hughes (1986), who proposed four categories to identify the stages of children's understanding.

1. Idiosyncratic – what the child records is not recognisable, although it has meaning for the child. It is possible to distinguish a pattern relating the objects to the representation.

2. Pictographic – what the child records is a representation of the objects and their number in pictures of the objects themselves.

3. Iconic – what the child records is a representation of the number of objects but does not include depicting the objects themselves.

4. Symbolic – what the child records shows the beginnings of connections between symbols and the number of objects; this may include using numerals (though not necessarily correctly) corresponding to the actual number of objects.

Penny Munn (1994) also looked at children's recording of quantity, and she grouped their marks into six categories.

1. Conventionally used numerals – numerals are used to represent number quantities.

2. Iconically used numerals – numerals are used to show the quantities, eg, using 22 to represent two.

3. Hieroglyphs – these are invented symbols which are not clearly identifiable to others but are meaningful to the child.

4. Tally marks – each mark represents one of the items counted.

5. Pictograms – these are pictures of the items showing the quantity.

6. Pretend writing – this looks like attempts to write letters and possibly words to describe the quantity.

Carruthers and Worthington (2005) created five categories after collecting hundreds of children's mark-making examples over a number of years.

1. Dynamic – marks that are lively and suggestive of action, with a freshness and spontaneity.

2. Pictographic – children try to represent something they can see in front of them.

3. Iconic – children use marks based on one-to-one counting. These are often marks that they have devised, in place of the things they are counting or calculating.

4. Written – children use letter-like marks or words.

5. Symbolic – children use standard numerals and mathematical symbols.

Critical question

»   *Re-read the three different categorisations of mark marking by Hughes, Munn, and Carruthers and Worthington. Identify the key similarities and differences between the researchers' views of mark making. Which classification would you find helpful to use with children's mark making in order to plan the next steps for their learning?*

Comment

You may find the work of Carruthers and Worthington helpful, as it offers a wide range of ways of categorising children's marks and separates writing from symbols; or perhaps you find Munn's classification most useful as it offers the largest number of categories.

Assessing children's mark-making skills

This can be difficult as you are not making a judgement about whether a child has made a correct mark; you may find it helpful to use the research categories detailed above to analyse the kinds of marks a child is making and plan the next appropriate learning experiences and opportunities for them.

INTERNATIONAL PERSPECTIVE

Writing numerals

In different countries the need for children to write down numerals and the age at which they are expected to do so varies. In Norway children attend kindergarten until the age of six, when they start school. They are not asked to write down numerals or to practise writing them. If children want to write numerals and ask to be shown how, then adults will facilitate this learning, but there is no pressure to do formal recording of any sort. By contrast, in China, perhaps as a by-product of having a language that is not phonically based, much of the early learning in nursery schools is by rote, through practising skills over and over again until children have memorised the skill and can write without hesitation. Children in China are taught how to record numbers early and are expected to practise writing numbers in the same way as they practise writing the language. For homework they are often given pages of repetitive exercises in writing numbers and letters. In the UK, pressures are returning to the mathematics curriculum at all levels for early recording and more learning of facts by rote.

Critical question

» *Review the current expectation for mathematics recording in the Early Years. How does this compare with the international perspectives? Which approach do you feel is the most appropriate and why?*

Comment

Expectations for mathematics recording are likely to change continually. But what is always important is children's understanding of what they commit to memory. Committing facts to memory can help to develop speed and efficiency in mathematics, but knowledge without understanding is not conducive to future development. For example, if a child knows the times tables but does not understand the underlying principles, it can actually be a barrier to future mathematical learning.

Play environments to facilitate mathematical mark making

These are activities that encourage children to make mathematical marks as a natural part of the play theme. The following should not be viewed as an exhaustive list but as a starting point for other creative ideas. The key is to make the mathematical rationale central, rather than the social aspect of play, which will continuously be present as part of the environment. Shops of different kinds are a good idea if children are provided with sufficient stimuli to support their play.

Shoe shop

Idea

This environment gives children the opportunity to use numbers in a different context. Shoe sizes are based on the length of the 'last', a wooden foot-shaped template over which leather could be shaped into a shoe. The length of a last was originally measured in an old unit called a barleycorn (approximately one third of an inch). The smallest practical size was defined to be size zero. This is not a formally standardised system. Nowadays shoe sizes in the UK are given in either this old system or the Continental system, which can be used to introduce children to larger numbers. Counting shoe boxes, ordering the sizes of shoes and measuring the feet of customers are all possible activities in this environment.

Equipment

Pairs of clean old shoes or shoes that the children have made themselves in various sizes; boxes for displaying the shoes on shelves or tables; a till and money for making sales; labels for the prices of items in the shop; clipboards, pens and paper for taking inventory of stock; bags to put purchases in when shoes are sold.

Outcomes

Children will talk about the size of shoes needed and record purchases, shoe prices and the number of shoes in stock for the inventory. They will record mathematical marks and generally talk about numbers in the context of the shop.

Builder's yard

Idea

This is an excellent activity for the outdoors and may appeal particularly to children who have been observed using a transporting schema in their play. Children may need some input informing them what a builder's yard actually does.

Equipment

Hard hats, tools, clipboards, pens and pencils, rulers, bits of wood, builder's trays, bricks, wheelbarrows, screws, nails, bags of sand, paint and brushes, and anything else that can be found to make the environment more realistic.

Outcomes

Children will visit the yard to collect building materials and can be encouraged to make lists of their purchases. Children can take their purchases away, or a delivery service could be introduced. Those working in the yard will need to keep track of their stock, and this will involve counting and recording. The children acting as customers will identify the items and the quantity of each item they need before making purchases. This could be set up as a 'cash-less' environment, with customers holding accounts which need to be recorded. Playing in this novel environment will extend children's experiences and stimulate their thinking.

Skittles

Idea

Games like skittles or ten-pin bowling can be a useful way of encouraging children to record their scores. Playing such games can be a simple and easy way to create a fun environment that children might already be familiar with.

Equipment

Lane marked out with bricks or similar barriers; ten pins per lane; balls; a scoring card or board, either one card for each child or a large easel with pens and paper.

Outcomes

Children record their scores in a variety of ways and talk about the number of pins they have knocked down and the number still to be knocked over. This environment can involve counting, calculating and mark making all in one activity.

In addition, the activities in any of the previous play environment sections could be adapted to encourage children to record their mathematical ideas.

Extend your subject knowledge

Laws associated with calculations

» *Commutative law*

This law says that numbers can be swapped around in a calculation and the answer will be the same. For instance, when adding two numbers a and b, we have $a + b = b + a$, eg, $4 + 3 = 3 + 4 = 7$.

And, when multiplying, we have $a \times b = b \times a$, eg, $4 \times 5 = 5 \times 4 = 20$.

The commutative law does not work for subtraction or division.

» *Associative law*

This law says that it doesn't matter how the numbers are grouped in a calculation. For instance, when adding three numbers a, b and c, we have $(a + b) + c = a + (b + c)$, eg, $(5 + 2) + 4 = 5 + (2 + 4)$.

And, when multiplying, $(a \times b) \times c = a \times (b \times c)$, eg, $(3 \times 4) \times 2 = 3 \times (4 \times 2)$.

This law does not work for subtraction or division.

» *Distributive law*

This law says that for three numbers a, b and c, $a \times (b + c) = a \times b + a \times c$.

For example, $3 \times (2 + 4) = 3 \times 2 + 3 \times 4 = 18$.

Which laws have been used in each of the following calculations?

(a) $(48 + 21) + 79 = 48 + (21 + 79) = 48 + 100 = 148$

(b) $(19 \times 5) \times 20 = 19 \times (5 \times 20) = 19 \times 100 = 1900$

(c) $4 \times 87 \times 25 = 4 \times 25 \times 87 = (4 \times 25) \times 87 = 100 \times 87 = 8700$

Use a mathematics dictionary to find out what 'infinity' means.

Critical learning points from this chapter

» Counting is a complex area for children to learn and is made up of a number of key components.

» Children need to understand the purpose of counting activities, and you need to explain to them that by counting they can tell how many items there are in a set.

» Children need opportunities to count a variety of items in different contexts in order to practise counting accurately.

» Children need guidance to help them develop their counting strategies in order to begin to calculate.

» Children need to be given opportunities to record quantity in their own way.

Critical reflection

Observe children counting and note how they keep track of the items they have counted. What do you notice about the marks that children make to record quantity? Can you use one of the sets of categories described in this chapter to assist you in analysing the marks? How might this information be used to plan the next steps for each child's learning?

Listen carefully to children's counting in play situations. Again, how might you use this information to assess their skills and plan the next steps in learning?

Consider creating a play environment that has a clear mathematical focus to encourage children to count and record their own reflections as part of the play.

Taking it further

Anghileri, J (2000) *Teaching Number Sense*. London: Continuum.

> In particular, chapter 2 focuses on counting.

Gelman, R and Gallistel, C (1978) *The Child's Understanding of Number*. Ambridge, Massachusetts: Harvard University Press.

> This book details how children acquire their understanding of number.

Haylock, D and Cockburn, A (2008) *Understanding Mathematics for Young Children*. London: Sage.

> In particular, chapter 2 focuses on number and counting.

References

Burningham, J (1992) *The Shopping Basket*. London: Red Fox Picture Books.

Butterworth, B (1999) *The Mathematical Brain*. London: Macmillan.

Carpenter, T and Moser, J (1984) The Acquisition of Addition and Subtraction Concepts in Grade One through Three. *Journal for Research in Mathematics Education*, 15(3): 179–202.

Carruthers, E and Worthington, M (2005) Making Sense of Mathematical Graphics: The Development of Understanding Abstract Symbolism. *European Early Childhood Education Research Journal*, 13(1): 57–79.

Frantz, R L (1964) Visual Experience in Infants: Decreased Attention to Familiar Patterns Relative to Novel Ones. *Science,* 146: 668–70.

Fuson K C (1988) *Children's Counting and Concepts of Number*. New York: Springer-Verlag.

Gelman, R and Gallistel, C (1978) *The Child's Understanding of Number*. Ambridge, Massachusetts: Harvard University Press.

Ginsburg, H (1977) *Children's Arithmetic: The Learning Process*. New York: Van Nostrand Company.

Hughes, M (1986) *Children and Number*. Oxford: Blackwell.

Maclellan, E (1997) The Importance of Counting, in Thompson, I (ed) *Teaching and Learning Early Number*. Buckingham: Open University Press.

Munn, P (1994) The Early Development of Literacy and Numeracy Skills. *European Early Childhood Education Research Journal,* 2(1): 5–18.

Munn, P (1997) Writing and Number, in Thompson, I (ed) *Teaching and Learning Early Number,* pp 89–96. Buckingham: Open University Press.

Wynn, K (1992) Evidence Against Empiricist Accounts of the Origins of Numerical Knowledge. *Mind and Language,* 7: 315–32.

3 Space, the final frontier

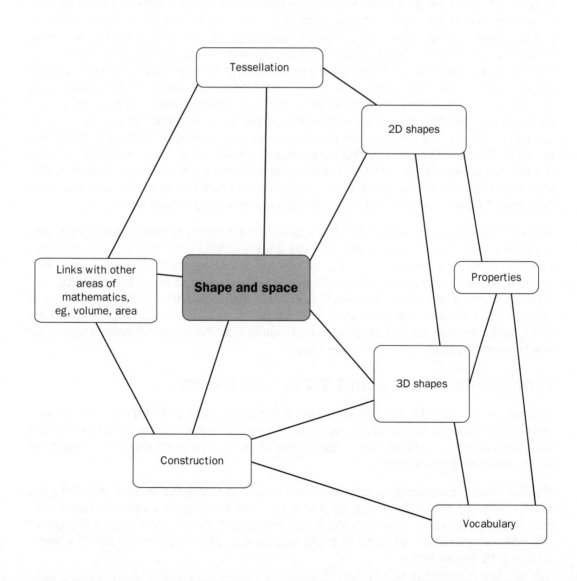

- Tessellation
- 2D shapes
- Links with other areas of mathematics, eg, volume, area
- **Shape and space**
- Properties
- 3D shapes
- Construction
- Vocabulary

Introduction

This chapter looks at shape and space, unpacks the essential subject knowledge you need, and explores some ways to engage young children with this aspect of mathematics. Shape and space is often seen as an easy area of mathematics, because shapes are all around us and so we might expect that everyone will be familiar with the terms and concepts. There can be assumptions about children's knowledge in this area, and perhaps a belief that it is not as demanding or difficult as other areas of mathematics. However, learning correct usage of the vocabulary of shape and space is crucial in helping children to gain a good geometrical sense, leading to a genuine understanding of the properties of shapes and space.

Young children's experiences with shape and space

Young children constantly explore the space around them as soon as they begin to interact with the world. They explore parts of their own body, other people's fingers, and things they come into contact with through touch, taste, sight and smell. They use all their senses to support them and help them make sense of what they are encountering. Children's early explorations are linked to developing their knowledge and understanding of the world around them, and are therefore also linked closely to early scientific development. Movements that young children make help them to explore objects in the space around them. Combining visual experiences with physical movements and touch assists children in developing their spatial knowledge. Young children enjoy putting objects inside containers and taking them out again. This can be seen as part of an enveloping or enclosing/containing schema in their play. Children also enjoy putting things together, building up towers and then watching the structures separate as they fall. The learning that arises from such activities is associated with language used by adults, other children and, later, themselves. These experiences help children develop initial mathematical skills and knowledge about space.

Shapes of things we can see or touch are usually too complex to describe, except in very rough terms, eg, 'the shell is a bit round' or 'the stairs are straight and they go up at an angle'. However, some objects have particular names for describing their shape. It is important to make available examples of many different two-dimensional (2D) and three-dimensional (3D) shapes for children to explore, such as equilateral triangles, tetrahedrons, squares and cubes, so that children can generalise their properties. It is also important to explore the relationship between 3D and 2D shapes and look at how the shapes of some faces of an object determine the shape of the other faces.

How children learn about shapes and space

Children learn about the differences between shapes by playing with them, building with them, drawing around them, combining them, making pictures with them, printing with them and rolling with them, and by talking about their experiences with adults, who can help put these experiences into words.

Children need to investigate shapes, large and small, manufactured and natural, and get a feel for the properties of these shapes. Rather than just learning the names of shapes, children need to learn about what each shape can and cannot do, and which shapes fit together and which shapes don't. Because of these factors, it is often helpful for children to begin exploring 3D shapes first.

Initially, children may not be able to verbalise why a shape is, for example, a circle or a triangle, although they seem to have an understanding of the shape as a whole (van Hiele, 1986), much as they understand that a table is a table in all its diverse forms. On the other hand, a young child may just focus on a single aspect such as 'pointiness', without seeing the shape as a whole or noticing other important properties.

Necessary vocabulary

Right from the beginning, it is important that you use the correct terms to help children develop their mathematical vocabulary. Once these terms are learnt, they don't need to be relearned at a later stage. It is therefore essential for you to know and use the correct terms at all times while you engage in appropriate discussion with children about their explorations. One key point about the names of shapes, whether 2D or 3D, is that they can tell you the number of sides the shape has and what kind of shape it is. For example, 'tri' means three, 'quad' means four, 'pent' means five, 'hex' means six, 'hept' means seven, 'oct' means eight, and so on. A shape name can also tell you whether the shape is 2D or 3D. For example, 'gon' comes from 'polygon', which means a many-sided plane or 2D shape with straight sides; 'polyhedra' are 3D shapes with plane faces, so names ending in 'hedron' are 3D shapes. The names are important labels for the objects, and small children can cope with these names very well, so there is no need to try to simplify things for them. Adults working with young children need to know the correct names themselves, or know where to access that information.

Not just regular shapes

Often the sets of shapes available in settings and schools contain mainly regular shapes. For instance, triangles are usually only presented as equilateral (with all sides equal and all internal and external angles equal). There is also a tendency to present the triangle in just one view.

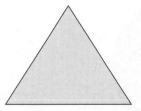

As a result, some children have difficulty seeing the following examples as triangles, because they don't look exactly the same as the triangles initially presented to them.

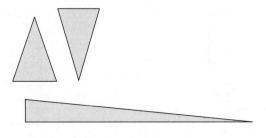

It is very important for children to learn to identify shapes by their properties, rather than just recognising presentations of regular shapes. The task of identifying shapes by their properties has often been part of tests at Key Stage 1.

Critical question

» *This activity is for you to have a go at, but you could also use it with a group of able children. How many triangles can you see in this picture?*

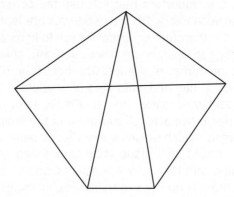

You will be using your knowledge about the properties of triangles to assist you with this task.

Solid or 3D shapes and their names

Three-dimensional (3D) shapes are so called because they have three dimensions – a height, a width and a depth.

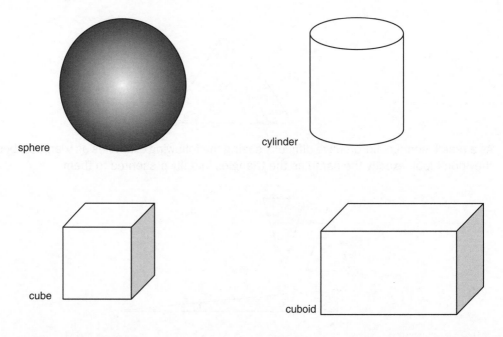

sphere

cylinder

cube

cuboid

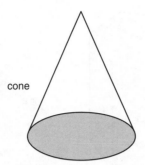

cone

Pyramids

Pyramids are 3D shapes which have a polygon for the base and triangular faces that meet at one vertex. The examples shown below are a hexagonal pyramid, a square pyramid and a pentagonal pyramid.

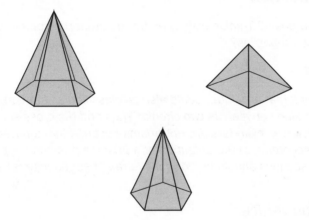

Prisms

A prism is a solid 3D shape with two identical, parallel bases and whose other faces are all rectangular. A prism has the same cross-section all along its length; if you cut slices along a side between the bases, you will see that all slices have the same shape and size. The name of the prism is taken from the shape of the base.

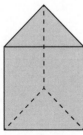

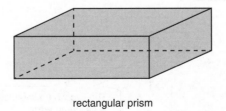

rectangular prism

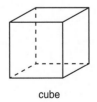

cube

triangular prism

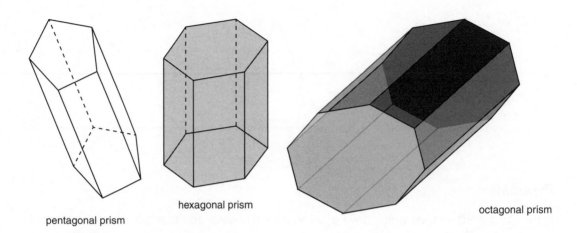

pentagonal prism

hexagonal prism

octagonal prism

Critical question

» *Is a cylinder a prism? Think carefully about the properties of a prism. Does a cylinder have all these properties?*

Comment

You might think that a cylinder could also be classified as a prism, because you could cut along the side between its two circular ends and the cross-sections would remain the same. However, cylinders are not prisms because the non-base sides are not flat but curved. According to the definition of a prism, a prism is a type of polyhedron, so all the cross-sections should be polygons (straight-edged figures) and all sides should be flat.

Faces, edges and vertices

All 3D shapes have faces, edges and vertices (plural of vertex, or corner).

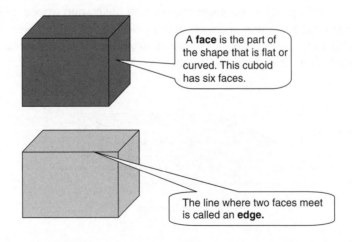

A **face** is the part of the shape that is flat or curved. This cuboid has six faces.

The line where two faces meet is called an **edge.**

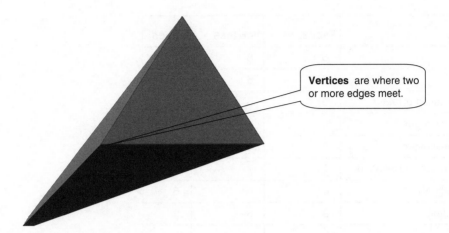

Vertices are where two or more edges meet.

Platonic solids

The platonic solids are 3D shapes where each face is the same regular polygon and the same number of faces meet at each vertex (corner). There are only five such shapes: the cube, tetrahedron, octahedron, dodecahedron and icosahedron. These 3D shapes have faces that are squares, equilateral triangles (triangles with all sides of equal length) or regular pentagons (five-sided polygons whose sides and angles are all equal).

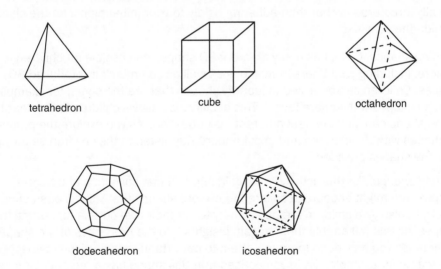

tetrahedron   cube   octahedron

dodecahedron   icosahedron

Euler's rule

Leonhard Euler (1707–83) was a Swiss mathematician who is particularly famous for his studies of polyhedra. He discovered a rule about the relationship between the numbers of vertices, faces and edges in each shape:

number of vertices + number of faces − number of edges = 2

Shape	Faces	Vertices	Edges
cube	6	8	12
cuboid	6	8	12
square-based pyramid	5	5	8
triangular prism	5	6	9
hexagonal prism	8	12	18
hexagonal-based pyramid	7	7	12
tetrahedron	4	4	6
octahedron	8	6	12
dodecahedron	12	20	30
icosahedron	20	12	30

Specific adult-led activities for exploring 3D shapes

The following are activities that an adult can plan and prepare for a small group of children to encourage them to look closely at 3D shapes and get familiar with the properties of the shapes through exploration and talk. Although these are adult-led activities, they don't have to be formally structured; rather than adhering rigidly to your initial plans, let the children's interest guide the activities.

- *Naming shapes*. Collect as many different 3D shapes as possible for children to explore, including containers from shops as well as commercially produced 3D shapes. Children can be asked to identify shapes that are the same; for example, 'find all shapes with square faces'. This activity also allows children to see that the same shape can look and feel different. Ask questions as you explore the properties of shapes with the children and, most importantly, listen to the children as they play with the shapes provided.

- *Sorting shapes*. For this activity, you again need a large collection of different shapes. You might encourage children to explore shapes that will roll or stack together; also give children the opportunity to set their own criteria for sorting the shapes, as this will enable them to gain insights into the properties of the shapes. Sometimes you may need to prompt them to pay attention to particular aspects of the shape; for example, 'Have you noticed that this shape has a rectangular face? Can you find another shape that has a face like this?'

- Prepare a feely bag filled with 3D shapes for children to explore. You can have either adults or the children describing the shapes for others to name.

- Collect different types of packaging for children to explore. Ask questions such as: 'Would these containers stack in a shop?', 'How much would it take to fill this container?' (linking with the concept of volume), 'What is stored in this kind of packaging?', 'Which packages have you seen before?'

- Spend time opening out and remaking shapes with children, demonstrating and talking about how a 3D shape can unfold into a 2D shape that looks quite different.

- Use blocks to construct different shapes and draw them to show how they fit together. Describe what the shapes look like so that children hear words such as straight, round, corner and flat.

- Have children look at what various 3D shapes can do – eg, roll, stack or fit together. This is a good activity to do outdoors with big shapes (differentiating this from the sorting activity described above, which is better undertaken indoors).

- Introduce tetrahedrons along with triangular prisms, squares with cubes, circles with cylinders, etc., so that children can relate and generalise the properties of 2D and 3D shapes.

- *Create shape walks*. Place shapes along a walk in the setting for children to find. Children can be given containers in which to put the shapes they have found and bring them back to explore in more detail later; alternatively, you could ask them to record which shapes they have seen.

- Search for corners and put a toy in every corner.

- Play games like 'I spy' or 'I am thinking of...' in which the children guess shapes.

Activities as part of continuous provision

In addition to specifically planned activities, there should be resources available in locations around the setting from which the children can choose, enabling them to explore shape and space.

- Provide materials such as boxes and other containers for children to construct their own models; this is sometimes referred to as 'junk modelling'.

- Provide access to construction materials, not just commercially produced kinds but also other collections of materials, that children can explore through play.

- Provide children with an extensive collection of 3D objects for exploring and building. Include large objects such as blocks, cardboard boxes and crates, as well as smaller objects such as sets of small bricks, construction kits and shaped blocks.

- Provide equipment for climbing and for sliding, rolling and stacking. This links to play schemas of transporting, containing, positioning and connecting.

- Provide modelling materials such as damp sand, dough, clay and modelling clay.

- Post shapes into posting boxes, either bought or home-made.

Play environments for children to explore 3D shapes

Different kinds of play environments provide children with opportunities to explore specific aspects of mathematics as well as to use mathematical language appropriately and reinforce their skills. As a teacher, you need to be aware of how children might exploit these opportunities for incidental reinforcement of skills such as counting or for learning new ideas that arise naturally in the play context. Although initially you may set up an area for children to explore, it is important that they be able to add to and develop the environment as they play, changing the emphasis according to their needs and interests. The following ideas are meant to provide starting points for creating your own play environments.

Box-packing company

Idea

Set up a play area as a box-packing company.

Equipment

Supply the area with cardboard boxes of different shapes and sizes and objects that need to be packed. Also provide address labels and possibly a wheeled cart for delivering parcels. You could make the area more inviting for children to explore by displaying some large maps of the area and a list of charges for delivering packages of different sizes. You could also provide overalls and caps for the packers and a machine for clocking into and out of work to make the environment more realistic. The scale and tasks of the environment could be varied – for example, set up a mini packing firm, with small boxes and tiny objects to pack; or develop a role for someone who checks the boxes before they are sent out (provide a clipboard and pen for the child playing this role). This is a particularly good environment to explore around holidays when gifts are sent out, eg, Christmas with presents or Easter with eggs.

Outcomes

Observe the children's behaviours and listen to their talk to see if they understand which shapes will stack and how to stack boxes of different shapes and sizes so that they won't fall over. Also observe children counting items naturally and recording quantities in their own way. Children may wish to change the play environment to suit their own interests, and adults should allow this to occur. For example, children may want to collect various items to fill the boxes or arrange the boxes in different patterns; this will give you many opportunities to discuss different mathematical ideas with the children.

Architect's office

Idea

Make an area into an architect's office. Before they begin to explore the play environment, explain to the children what an architect is and what architects do.

Equipment

Pictures of building exteriors and interiors, plans and elevations; drawing equipment and art easels or picture stands, so that children can make their own drawings of a newly designed school or house; a variety of pens and pencils; a digital camera for children to capture pictures of interesting local buildings to add to the display in the office, which is useful for stimulating discussion among children and between adults and children; possibly also construction materials so that the children can make models of the buildings they are designing.

Outcomes

Children will draw buildings that they have seen or are designing. Perspective is a difficult aspect of drawing 3D objects, but even at an early age children will try to show all sides in the same drawing; you may also find that, after looking at real plans, some children will draw a bird's eye view. These drawing activities will give children opportunities to use rulers and set squares. To develop their 3D visualisation skills, which are so important for later learning of geometric ideas, ask children about the views of their buildings, whether they could build a 3D model of their design, and what would be the functions of their buildings.

Plane or 2D shapes

Common two-dimensional (2D) shapes that children will encounter are polygons, which are made up of straight lines that meet to form a closed shape. The word 'polygon' comes from Greek, with 'poly' meaning many and 'gon' meaning angle.

Squares, rectangles and oblongs

The terms used for these related shapes can cause a lot of difficulty for both children and adults, so let's have a look at the definitions in more detail. All of these shapes are quadrilaterals, which means they have four sides.

Squares are polygons that have four sides all of the same length and four internal right angles (ie, each angle is 90 degrees).

Rectangles are quadrilaterals whose four sides consist of two pairs of parallel and equal sides; rectangles also have four internal right angles.

Critical question

» *Can a rectangle be a square? To answer the question, think carefully about the properties of each and the relationships between them.*

Comment

According to the definitions above, a square can also be a rectangle, as a square has two pairs of parallel equal sides and four internal right angles. However, a rectangle may not be a square, as not all of its sides are necessarily of the same length. So we can say that a square is a specific type of rectangle. If a child brings you a square when you asked for a rectangle, they are correct.

Oblongs are quadrilaterals which have four internal right angles and two pairs of parallel equal sides, with the two pairs being of different lengths.

From the definitions, you can see that rectangles can be oblongs but squares do not meet the definition of an oblong. Putting it another way, an oblong is a type of rectangle, and a square is a type of rectangle, but a square is not an oblong because its sides are all of the same length.

Tessellation

A tessellation is formed when 2D shapes are placed in a repeating pattern to cover a surface so that there are no gaps between the individual shapes; an example would be covering a floor or wall with tiles. Tessellations can be formed by using only one shape or by combining two or more shapes.

Critical question

» *Take a box of 2D shapes and see which shapes fit into each of the categories below. See if you can work out what it is about the shapes that will not tessellate.*

Shapes that will tessellate with the same shape	Shapes that will tessellate in combination with other shapes	Shapes that will not tessellate

Regular tessellations are composed of identical copies of a regular polygon with equal sides and angles. The internal angles of the regular polygon must divide evenly into 360 degrees. This means that each vertex must have the same number of shapes meeting there. For example, in the following illustration of tessellating squares, the point (vertex) in the centre has four corners meeting there, and the corner of each square is a 90 degree angle; notice that $4 \times 90 = 360$.

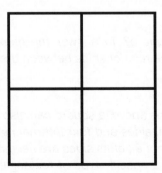

If you were tessellating with equilateral triangles, then there would be six triangles meeting at every vertex, each with internal angles of 60 degrees. Notice that 6 × 60 = 360; that is why equilateral triangles tessellate.

You can have semi-regular tessellations, which are made by combining different shapes in a repeating pattern so that they fit together without gaps.

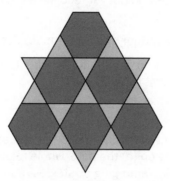

Some shapes won't tessellate. For example, a regular pentagon has internal angles of 108 degrees; 108 does not divide evenly into 360, so you cannot get a regular tessellation from pentagons.

Around the vertex in the middle there is a gap where the shapes cannot meet, because 108 + 108 + 108 = 324, not 360 (the gap is 36 degrees).

FOCUS ON RESEARCH

Van Heile levels

There is a considerable amount of research on the acquisition of knowledge and under-standing about shape and space. The most well-known writer is van Heile, who classified geometrical learning into a series of five levels (van Heile, 1986).

1. Shapes are recognised by their global appearance, without awareness of their prop-erties. Children use words such as 'square' or 'triangle' but do not focus on proper-ties such as equality of sides.

2. Properties of shapes are recognised and analysed, but children do not explicitly inter-relate shapes or properties. They know that all the angles of a rectangle are right angles, but they do not explicitly recognise that a square is also a rectangle.

3. Relationships between shapes and properties are recognised; children know that every square is a rectangle, but they cannot yet form sequences of deductions to justify their arguments.

4. Children can now put together chains of arguments to deduce one geometrical statement from another, but they do not yet recognise the need for rigour in aspects of geometrical proof.

5. Children can now rigorously analyse and compare deductive systems.

The levels are not evenly spaced across the knowledge to be acquired. For children in the Early Years, the focus is on the first two or three levels.

Other theories

Australian researchers Owens et al (2001) looked at the acquisition of geometrical knowledge in a different way, focusing on (a) the part–whole relationship, and (b) orientation and motion. Children begin with using emerging strategies, putting pieces together to see what shapes they might make; at this stage a child is able to match a name with a simple shape. At the next stage, with perceptual strategies, the child can recognise whole shapes used to build a picture and can describe similarities and differences between shapes. As children develop pictorial imagery strategies, they can separate parts of shapes from the whole and match parts from one shape to others; they can identify similarities between different representations of the same shape. When children move on to pattern and dynamic imagery strategies, they can discuss patterns and movements associated with combining shapes and relationships between shapes. Finally, children develop efficient strategies, with which they can assess images and plan the effective use of properties of shapes and composite units to generate shapes; they are also able to describe the effective use of shape properties to generate new shapes.

Again, for the Early Years, the initial strategies are the most important.

Critical question

» *Re-read the descriptions above of the two different approaches to thinking about the development of geometrical knowledge and skills. What do you see as the key differences, and how might those affect teaching practice?*

Comment

An important part of the work of Owens et al is the movement of shapes and the difference that makes to children's ability to identify properties; van Heile, on the other hand, treats shapes as more static. For children, seeing shapes in different orientations as having the same properties is crucial for developing understanding of concepts such as 'quadrilateralness'.

Specific adult-led activities for exploring 2D shapes

The following are activities for you to do with children. You should ask and answer questions about the shapes, encouraging children to use the correct terminology. These are designed to be short introductory activities to engage children's interest, although depending on the age group you are working with, your school/setting may expect you to lead more formally planned sessions.

- *Naming shapes*. Make a collection of 2D shapes for children to explore. Children can be asked to find a specific shape or pick any shape and tell the rest of the group about it. What do they notice about the shape? Does it have straight edges? How many corners?

- *Sorting shapes*. Collect a variety of 2D shapes, both regular and non-regular, for children to sort. This gives children an opportunity to explore, for instance, the 'triangleness' of triangles of different appearances, so that children learn to identify the common properties of specific shapes.

- Walk along in straight-line crocodiles and then in a curve or zigzag path. Encourage children to see the difference between curved, straight and wiggly lines. This is the kind of activity that can be undertaken when children are in transition between other activities or moving outside as a small group; use the change of location as a stimulus for mathematical thinking.

- Prepare a feely bag filled with 2D shapes for children to explore. Feely bags are familiar equipment in settings and can be used for all sorts of games. Either you or some of the children can describe the shapes for others to name. This activity again focuses on identifying the properties of shapes, so you should always include some non-regular shapes to help promote understanding of the essential properties of specific shapes.

- Fill small plastic bottles or sauce dispensers with water, and then, using big circular hand movements, squirt the water on to large sheets of paper or on paving slabs outdoors. Talk with the group of children about the shapes created.

- *Create shape walks*. Place shapes along a walk for children to find. See the adult-led activities for 3D shapes.

- Ask children to sort a collection of pasta shapes and find all the spirals; then look for more spirals in shells and sunflowers, for example.

- Use chalk to draw shapes outdoors and have children hop around the lines or jump inside the shapes. Children can also be asked to go and find a particular shape and stand in it; this reinforces specific mathematical vocabulary.

- Make tessellations using various 2D shapes, both regular and irregular.

- Play games like 'I spy' or 'I am thinking of...' in which the children guess shapes.

- Cut sponges into different shapes for printing.

- Make shaped biscuits to decorate. Cutters come in different shapes which the children can sort, use and talk about.

- Mark out large shapes on the floor. Children run round to music and have to stand inside a given shape when the music stops.

- Get children to move round to music and tell them that when the music stops, they must make a shape with their body or in collaboration with others.

Activities as part of continuous provision

The following are activities that could be integrated into the continuous provision in your setting. You can support the children's learning by, for example, reinforcing vocabulary, but children can also explore these activities on their own.

- Use 2D shapes to make pictures. This can be done as a table-top activity or with large shapes outdoors, and you can take pictures of the children's creations for discussion in adult-led activities or when reviewing the day-time activities with your group. The pictures can also be used to make labelled displays in the setting.

- Provide spaces both indoors and outdoors with various shapes marked out for children to fill in whatever way they like.

- Use chalk to draw shapes outdoors for children to play hop around the lines or jump inside the shapes.

- Squirt water from plastic water bottles using big circular hand movements, or draw shapes on outdoor walls with a bucket of water and a large brush. This is a particularly good activity for children to do outside in warmer weather.

Play environments for children to explore 2D shapes

Biscuit factory

Idea

Set up a play area as a biscuit company. You could do this in two different ways. One is as part of a cooking activity, which would need adult supervision if real biscuits are to be baked. The biscuits can be decorated and boxed as part of the activity. (Care is needed with any cooking activity – check for potential food allergies and parental consent to eat the ingredients used.) Alternatively, use play dough or similar materials to make biscuits which are not edible; again these can be decorated and boxed. This is a particularly good environment to explore around festival times or events when gifts are given.

Equipment

Resources for the cooking activity might include disposable hair nets and gloves, and aprons or protective clothing. You will need suitable biscuit cutters in various shapes and small boxes for packaging. You could make the area more inviting for children to explore by displaying pictures of biscuits from magazines and old cookbooks.

Outcomes

Children will cut out biscuits with biscuit cutters of various shapes or design their own biscuit shapes. They will see how many biscuits will fit into a box if packed carefully. Children can design patterns on their biscuits with straight or curved lines of icing. They will sort biscuits according to their shape properties.

Garden designer

Idea

This is a small play environment, using a builder's tray as the confines of the garden. Children can be left to freely explore the resources provided, or they could be given a brief that the garden must contain a certain number and type of elements. You could try both approaches when using this play environment.

Equipment

Resources can include a wide variety of items and materials that children can use to design patterns within their tray gardens.

Outcomes

Children will be able to design their own shape patterns in their gardens. They might make repeating and non-repeating patterns. This links with play schemas of connecting, enveloping, containing and enclosing. Discuss the advantages and disadvantages of different-shaped gardens and subsections of gardens. This activity also provides a good way to look at simple symmetry of shapes.

Mining or panning for shapes

Idea

This is a very simple activity which takes little preparation. In the classroom or outdoors, fill some containers with small rocks, among which you place small plane shapes for the children to mine. You could have each child working at a small container or several children around a larger container. Alternatively, fill a tray with water, sand and gravel, and hide small shapes within; children then pan for the shapes as though they are panning for gold.

Equipment

You would need containers, small rocks or something to represent rocks, and a collection of small plane shapes. You could supply each child with a miner's lamp made from a small light attached to a head-band. The whole play area could be made cave-like with some draped material in a corner of the room, and you could make it more exciting by using glowing shapes and a torch to help find the shapes. If you use magnetic shapes or shapes with velcro attached, a chart could be created to keep track of how many shapes each child has mined. For the panning environment, you would need a long deep tray, water, sand and gravel to fill it with, and a collection of small shapes.

Outcomes

Children can describe the shapes collected and sort them according to their properties. You could ask children to identify which shapes are the same and which are different.

Children could count the different shapes and compare their skills of mining or panning with others in the group. They might record the number of each shape mined or panned.

INTERNATIONAL PERSPECTIVE

Working with the child's own interests

In the Norwegian framework plan for the content and tasks of kindergartens, the focus is on following children's interests. Adults need to feel confident in their own subject knowledge in order to see the opportunities in the activities that children choose to do alongside the activities that are specifically planned or resourced. This is why the earlier part of this chapter focuses on understanding subject knowledge. Armed with this knowledge, adults will be able to work more intuitively with children and their interests and questions.

The outdoors is a key resource for stimulating children's interest in shape and space – for example, by collecting leaves, stones, seeds and twigs to make patterns, or sorting these into collections. In Norway children are often outdoors no matter what the weather is, but they are prepared for this by having suitable clothing. After the first snow, children are keen to explore activities associated with this event. They might start with drawing the snowmen that they will build. A basic snowman is made of two circles and a shape for the hat that the children design independently; they then put these shapes together to form their finished pictures of snowmen. Afterwards the children might carefully stick small pieces of white paper onto the snowman picture; the pieces of paper covering the snowman link shape with the measurement of area.

The outdoors is also an ideal environment for exploring the positional language associated with space and shape. Words such as 'in', 'on', 'under', 'between' and 'through' can be emphasised and discussed as children play with large equipment outdoors.

Collecting leaves can be an early introduction to symmetry. Can you fold a leaf so that one side covers the other?

Assessing children's skills

Can children:

- talk about the shapes of everyday objects;

- recognise simple 3D and 2D shapes (eg, cubes, squares, circles) by sight and begin to name them;

- match some shapes by recognising their similarities and orientation;

- recognise the properties of shapes so that they can identify regular and non-regular shapes;

- use positional language to describe the relationship between themselves and objects or between two objects?

Test your subject knowledge

1. Is a cube a prism?

2. Test yourself on the relationships between squares, rectangles and oblongs. According to its definition, which group(s) can a square belong to?

3. Which shapes are the platonic solids?

4. Can you name three shapes which will tessellate in a repeating pattern on their own (ie, not combined with another shape)?

Extend your subject knowledge

» Use a mathematics dictionary to look up the correct names of shapes before you introduce them to children.

» Have a large children's mathematics dictionary in the setting for children, as well as adults, to explore.

» Display posters of shapes in the setting that children and adults can use for reference.

Critical learning points from this chapter

» Language is key to describing shapes and space and the relationship between them.

» Using the correct mathematical terms from the beginning is very important for developing children's understanding.

» Concrete experiences of handling, exploring and describing shapes and space is essential for the development of understanding.

» Orientation of shapes is an important aspect of being able to identify their properties.

» There are many creative ways to stimulate children to explore the relationship between shapes and space.

Critical reflection

When working with young children to explore shapes and space, is it better to start with 2D shapes or 3D shapes? Why? What existing resources/equipment/environments are there in your setting/school that will allow children to explore shapes and the relationship with space?

Taking it further

Blinko, J (2000) *Shape, Space and Measure*. London: A&C Black.

> This book is specifically about shape and space.

Haylock, D and Cockburn, A (2008) *Understanding Mathematics for Young Children*. London: Sage.

> In particular, chapter 8 focuses on shape and space.

Montague-Smith, A and Price, A (2012) *Mathematics in the Early Years Education* (third edition). London: David Fulton.

> In particular, chapter 5 is about shape and space.

References

Owens, K, Reddacliff, C, Gould, P and McPhail, D (2001) Changing the Teaching of Space Mathematics, in Bobis, J, Perry, B and Mitchelmore, M (eds) *Numeracy and Beyond: Proceedings of the 24th Annual Conference of the Mathematics Education Research Group of Australasia*, pp 402–9. Sydney: MERGA.

van Hiele, P (1986) *Structure and Insight: A Theory of Mathematics Education*. New York: Academic Press.

4 Are we nearly there yet?

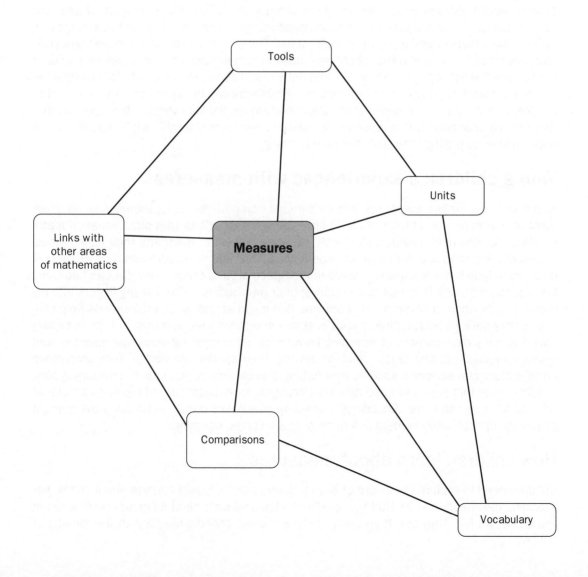

Introduction

Measures are the means of comparing things, either directly or, where this is not possible, by using units. This is the aspect of mathematics that people use most often in everyday life. Most of the time we either perform a direct comparison or use estimates to make a judgement about quantities of liquid, length, distance, weight or time. For example, we make comparisons between the money in our bank account and the cost of things we want to buy; or we estimate the amount of paint that we will need to paint a room, the length of cotton required to mend a hole in a sweater, or the amount of fuel we should have in our car in order to travel a certain distance.

This chapter looks at children's concept of time and distance, as well as some other measures, and discusses why these measures can be difficult for children to understand. Measures often become a source of frustration between adults and children, particularly around the passage of time, which is one of the hardest measures for children to develop a full appreciation of. Adults sometimes use the phrase 'Just a minute' to indicate an amount of time; but this can range from a few seconds to never, depending on what the children have asked and whether the adults intend to agree to the request. The common question 'Are we there yet?' also illustrates the kind of difficulty children have with measures of time. Children also tend to measure the passage of time by informal units that they are familiar with, for example the number of sleeps to a big event like a birthday, Christmas or a family holiday. This shows that children are trying to make sense of the situation through linking events to time periods that they already understand. This process can take children a considerable while, and they need opportunities to practise the skills they are learning.

Young children's experiences with measures

Young children explore measures initially through comparison, using themselves as a key point of reference – Am I taller than X? Am I younger than Y? As with other areas of mathematical development, children start with the world closest to them and their experiences, before moving on to a wider range of experiences. The natural movements that young children make help them to explore objects in the space around them – How far can I stretch? Can I reach that toy? This includes exploring their own bodies – Can I fit my fingers into my mouth? What about a whole hand? Funny as this might sound, such explorations help children's very early understanding of shape, space and measures, and this, in turn, is closely linked to early development of scientific knowledge. By combining visual experiences with physical movements and touch, children develop their spatial knowledge. They then move on to explore play schemas such as enveloping or enclosing/containing. In enveloping play, children cover things and so need to make decisions, for example, about the size of material needed to cover the items. Enclosing/containing play might involve estimating the amount of something that could be held in a hand or in a selected container.

How children learn about measures

Children need to explore the extent of any measure, that is, where it starts and finishes. For example, they need to know that the length of a toy snake starts at its head and finishes at the end of its tail. They can then compare this specific snake's length with the lengths of

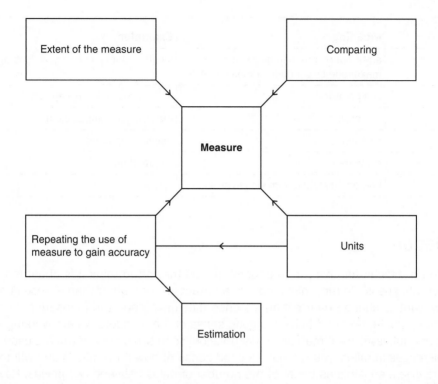

other snakes. From making such comparisons children can move on to measuring with units, which initially may be non-standard units such as bricks of different sizes laid along the snake's length. Then children move from using non-standard or arbitrary units of measurement towards understanding why there is a need for standardised units. This step requires careful discussion with children so that they appreciate the reason for having standardised measures. After this comes the choice of the most appropriate measuring instrument for each particular situation, and then children need to repeat its use to gain the skill of accurate measuring. The final step is developing the skill of estimation. For children to be able to estimate, they first need to have a sound understanding of the measure being employed.

Necessary vocabulary

Measures have their own vocabulary, which can sometimes be confusing for young children. Children may find words such as 'small' and 'big' difficult to use appropriately. They tend to use these labels to compare the overall sizes of objects, including as comparators of different kinds of measures; so they might use 'small' and 'big' in relation to height, or use these words for relative ages. 'Short' and 'tall' can also be confusing, as 'short' applies to vertical height as well as to horizontal lengths.

Word	Meaning	Examples
measure	use of a unit (non-standard or standard) to find a size or quantity	length, breadth, height, area, mass, weight, volume, capacity, temperature, time

Word	Meaning	Examples
quantity	any property that can be given a magnitude by counting or measuring	length, volume, capacity, weight, age
small	comparator	mass, area, volume, capacity
big	comparator	mass, area, volume, capacity
short	comparator	height, length, time
long	comparator	length, time
width	breadth, distance from side to side	length

Estimation

Estimation is difficult for children to understand, as they often think it is about making the most accurate guess. So they might look for an exact answer rather than a close guess, and they may want to change their estimates once they have done the measuring. In order to be able to estimate, we need to have a good sense of the measure we are working with. An example at adult level is estimating the distance between two places. If you are used to measuring distances in miles, you will have a good sense of how far a mile is and will therefore be able to give a sensible estimate of the number of miles between two places. However, if someone asks you to give the estimate in kilometres and you are unfamiliar with working with this unit of distance, you may find it difficult. This example shows that experience of a specific measure is required before estimation can take place.

FOCUS ON RESEARCH

Children need practice comparing measures of length, mass, volume or capacity, and time. To begin with, they make direct comparisons of one item with another and use mainly visual comparison for length and volume. With mass, they focus on the feel of weight to make comparisons between items. These means of comparison are not without difficulties, as can be seen from Piaget's experiments on conservation of length, volume and mass.

Conservation of length

In the first of three experiments, Piaget assessed children's understanding of the conservation of length. Conservation of length means that appreciation of the comparative lengths of two objects is unaffected by their relative positions or straightness.

The experimenter presents two rods to a child and asks: 'Are the rods the same length, or is one longer than the other?'

The experimenter then moves one of the rods with the child watching. The same question is asked again: 'Are the rods the same length, or is one longer than the other?'

An alternative format of the experiment uses pieces of string to represent the two equal lengths. The question remains the same: 'Are the pieces of string the same length, or is one longer than the other?'

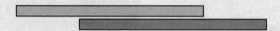

Conservation of volume

In the second experiment, Piaget assessed children's understanding of the conservation of liquid volume. In the first situation there are two identical containers with the same amount of liquid in each. The child is asked the question 'Does one container have more liquid in it than the other, or do they both have the same?'

Then the liquid from one of the containers is poured into a short but wide container in front of the child so they can see what is happening. They are asked the same question again: 'Does one container have more liquid in it than the other, or do they both have the same?'

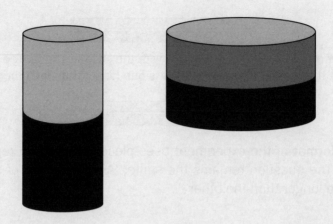

Conservation of mass

The third experiment focuses on mass. The child is shown two exactly identical rolls of modelling dough and is asked 'Does one cylinder have more modelling dough than the other, or do they both have the same?'

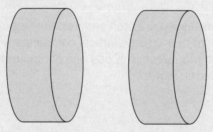

Then one cylinder is squashed into a pancake shape in front of the child so they can see what is happening. They are asked the same question again: 'Does one cylinder have more modelling dough than the other, or do they both have the same?'

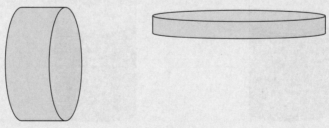

Outcomes from the experiments

Children either can see that the measures remain the same or they can't. Flavell, Miller and Miller (1993) write that a *young child tends to be fooled by the misleading perceptual appearance*. This is the case for children who are not able to conserve measures in the Piagetian experiments.

In these Piagetian experiments, children before the age of seven tend to be influenced by the visual appearance and do not conserve the measures. If children cannot conserve measures, then they will find comparisons of measures more difficult as they rely too much on the visual image. In estimating measures, children also need to be able to estimate length, mass or volume regardless of the containers or the physical presentation.

Understanding the strong influence of children's visual perception is important in helping us to understand their misconceptions. For example, in the diagram below the toy car is heavier than the block, but some children see the block as being heavier because it appears higher than the car and they are assuming that 'higher' is equivalent to 'more'.

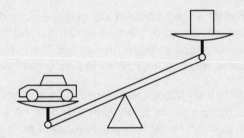

Conservation of area

One measure that young children explore in their play but are not taught directly about in Early Years mathematical education is area. Piaget also examined area in one of his conservation experiments. Two toy animals are each given a patch of grass to eat. At first the patches of grass are identical. The child is asked 'Do the toy animals have the same amount to eat, or does one have more than the other?'

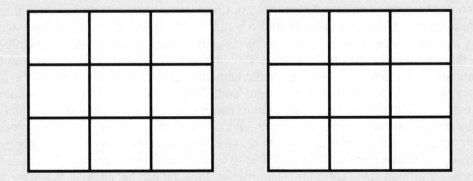

Then one of the patches of grass is rearranged and the child is again asked 'Do the toy animals have the same amount to eat, or does one have more than the other?'

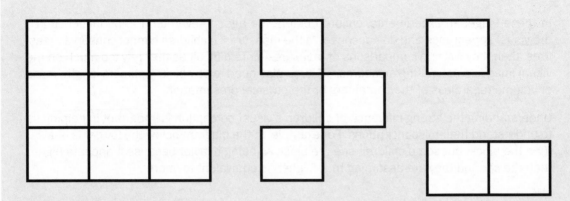

As in the previous experiments, young children are influenced by the visual appearance of the situations. They are also influenced by the format of the questions asked and by the fact that they are asked the same question more than once. The reason for this is that adults usually ask the same question more than once if the first answer was incorrect.

Young children explore area in their play through enveloping or covering things – for example, covering toys in a bed, hiding toys or themselves in a den, or collecting sticks to make the roof of a house. In such play, they are exploring measures of area when they decide on the quantity of materials needed to cover or envelop the chosen objects.

Non-standard and standard measures

The next stage after comparing measures directly is the use of non-standard measures such as cupfuls or steps or hand-widths, which are similar to some of the ancient measures. For example, to measure length, our ancestors used 'hand', which is the distance across the palm of the hand; this unit is still used today for the height of horses. Similarly, a cubit is the length between the elbow and the tip of the middle finger; this was the main unit of length in ancient Egypt. It wasn't until the eighteenth century that England established the standard measures that are still in use today, although we now actually use a mixture of metric and imperial units. Boulton-Lewis, Wilss and Mutch (1996) discuss the recommendation that children should begin by measuring with non-standard, sometimes called arbitrary, units, which is motivated by the belief that this will help children to recognise the need for a standard unit. They question the view that measuring with non-standard units will naturally lead to using standard measures, as they think that using non-standard units doesn't lead children to consider that they are 'really measuring' in the same way as they see adults doing it. In a study of Australian children in the first three years of school, Boulton-Lewis et al found that children preferred to use standard rather than non-standard units, even though they did not necessarily measure accurately. Consequently, they recommend that *children be encouraged to measure directly and indirectly with both standard measures and arbitrary units from the first year of school* (Boulton-Lewis, Wilss and Mutch, 1996, page 345). They suggest that this would make the activities involving measures more meaningful to the children. Nunes, Light and Mason (1993) found that using a ruler supported children's reasoning about length and improved their performance: children were *clearly profiting from the numerical representation available through the ruler* (Nunes et al, 1993, page 46). They go on to suggest ways of working with measures similar to those proposed by Boulton-Lewis et al (1996). Nunes et al also see benefits in working from the approaches to solving measurement problems that children bring with them to the classroom, as this would facilitate making the connection between the task of measuring and the meaning of measurement.

Critical question

» *Are standard measurement instruments or discrete non-standard units more effective in teaching children about measurement?*

Comment

As discussed above, this is a matter of debate between researchers, although what is clear is that most current curricula emphasise both approaches. Children therefore gain experience in using both non-standard and standard measures; however, through these they tend to gain instrumental understanding of the use of measures rather than a deep understanding of the meaning of measurement. They may also see differently the purpose of specific activities and not be able to make the connection between these classroom activities and the use of measuring in everyday life.

Critical question

» *What is the difference between volume and capacity?*

Comment

The volume of a solid is how much space it occupies. Capacity is the amount of liquid a container can hold when it is full.

Critical question

» *What is the difference between mass and weight?*

Comment

The mass of an object is a property of the object which remains constant unless you take part of the object away; for example, a ball of modelling dough could have a mass of 100g and this would remain constant unless you cut the ball in half, in which case the mass of each half would be 50g. The weight of an object, however, can change without the object being changed; it is a measure of the gravitational pull on the object. In everyday life we tend to use the terms mass and weight interchangeably, and also use the same units of measurement, grams and kilograms, for both. On the surface of the Earth, weight and mass are the same because there is little difference in the influence of gravity all over the world. Technically, however, weight should be measured in newtons (the units of force) rather than kilograms, and when talking about weight we should say that 'the book weighs the same as 200 grams' rather than 'the book weighs 200 grams'.

Time

Time is different from other measures in that we cannot see or touch it and therefore it is difficult to get a sense of its extent. Children also find it difficult to get a sense of the size of time units: minutes and hours are too long and seconds are too short for children to grasp their extent. Although adults tend to focus on teaching the skill of telling the time, clocks are not much good for measuring amounts of time that children can grasp. Keeping this in mind, we need to give children opportunities to use other kinds of timers, such as egg or sand timers, to help them get a sense of short time periods and integrate this with their experiences with longer periods such as weeks, months and years. In this way, children will simultaneously learn about the two important aspects of time: the passage of time and the telling or measuring of time.

With telling the time, start with times that children are familiar with, such as getting up, going to school or nursery, lunch times and home times. Initially children are typically introduced to an analogue clock and hour times. Analogue clocks are devices that have a round face with 12 hours marked and usually two hands that move over the face. The positions of the hour and minute hands show the time, which can be either 'am' or 'pm'. On a digital clock the display can show the 12-hour time with 'am' or 'pm' next to the numbers, or it can show the 24-hour time. Children are more likely to have experience of digital displays of time on electronic devices in the home, but some may have seen or own a watch with an analogue display. When teaching children how to tell the time, we generally move from whole hours to half past, then to quarter past and quarter to, and finally to times in between. When telling the time in English, we focus on times past and to the hour, but in countries such as Norway and Germany people also talk about past and to the half hour, so you could have five past the half past, for example.

Critical question

» *Write down as many words and phrases associated with time as you can.*

Comment

You are likely to have written down a wide range of words, which may include hour, minute and second as well as phrases such as 'just a minute', 'waste of time' or 'just in time'. The multitude of words and phrases associated with time illustrates the potential for young children to have already established various misconceptions about the passage of time based on everyday language. It also emphasises the need to talk about time with children and explore their understanding so that they will not only learn to tell the time using a clock but also understand the passage of time and how it is measured in the short and longer term.

Tools and units

A key aspect of measures is the use of different kinds of tools or measuring devices and the standard units that are associated with each of the measures. Young children find some of the standard measures difficult to use because they are so small; therefore it is easier to begin with the larger measures. An example of this is grams and kilograms: if you hold a gram weight in your hand, it doesn't really allow you to feel the 'heaviness' of the mass, but you can certainly feel the mass of a kilogram weight. Starting with the kilogram allows young children to make a direct physical comparison between objects and the kilogram. Similarly with centimetres and a metre; initially, making comparisons between various lengths and a metre stick is easier than comparing with centimetres. The key idea here is to look for equivalence, through finding objects less than, more than and about the same as the measure. When children begin to use the appropriate tools for measuring and to look at the standard units, they encounter the issue of reading scales, such as the markings on a ruler, measuring jug or weighing scales.

One of the problems children might have with rulers is that the scale doesn't always start at the end of the ruler, and children have to learn to look closely when deciding where to start measuring from; at first they may take the very end of the ruler, where there are no markings, as the start of the measure. Another difficulty is learning to start at zero, because the counting that they have encountered previously usually starts at 1; children may initially start measuring a length at a range of points along the ruler.

The numbers on some measuring scales become large very quickly, and so children's understanding of number, including place value, may not have caught up with the magnitudes shown on these scales. It is only through repeated use of a specific measuring tool that children will increase their ability to measure accurately.

Specific adult-led activities for exploring measures

The following are activities that an adult can plan and prepare for a small group of children to encourage them to look closely at various measures and get familiar with the idea of comparison through exploration and talk. Although these are adult-led activities, they don't have to be formally structured; rather than adhering rigidly to your initial plans, let the children's interest guide the activities.

- Show children a collection of toys and get them to compare the sizes of the toys by asking questions such as: Which one is the tallest? Which one is the shortest? Which one is taller than...? Children can start with comparing two toys and then move on to ordering the toys according to size.

- Do a 'people maths' activity, in which you use the children themselves as the resource for questions. With a small group of children, you could ask them to compare who is the tallest/shortest, who has the biggest feet or biggest hands, etc. (However, care is needed not to upset children who might be self-conscious about their size.)

- Collect different types of packaging and containers for children to explore the amounts that they can hold. This gives children practice in comparing volume and capacity, and can be helpful in developing children's understanding of equivalence and conservation of volume. Sand or other materials could be used to fill a range of containers to find out which one holds the most or least.

- Compare the masses of various objects by using a bucket balance or similar piece of equipment. This allows children to explore which object is heavier first by feeling the mass of each object in their hands and then by placing the objects on a balance. If children seem to hold the misconception that the higher object is heavier, then this can be discussed further and the misconception potentially remedied.

- Compare footsteps – have the children draw around their feet and cut out footsteps. You could supply them with other footsteps, such as those of adults in the setting, a fairy or a giant, a large animal and a small animal. The lengths and sizes of these footsteps can be compared and discussed.

- See how much the children can do while the sand runs out of an egg timer. First the children need to be shown how long it takes for the sand to flow from one side of the timer to the other. Then ask them to perform specific actions such as jumping, clapping or building towers.

- See how much the children can do while the water is dripping through a water clock. Water clocks allow specific amounts of water to flow out, depending upon the size of the hole in the bottom, and they provide another way of measuring time. Similar kinds of actions to those in the previous activity can be used here.

- Create a display of measure-related words to discuss with children. It is best if each display is focused on a specific measure. For example, if you focus on volume and capacity, the words on the display could include litre, cupful, teaspoon, millilitre, etc. You could use a display relating to the passage of time and the changing seasons to prompt discussion about observable changes in the environment; in this case the display could include pictures of the outdoor areas of the setting/school at different times of the year.

- Make porridge for the play environment of Goldilocks and the three bears (see play environments), and then order the portions of porridge in bowls of different sizes.

The making of porridge gives children opportunities to measure ingredients using cupfuls or standard measures.

• Knit or sew a scarf that can be used to measure lengths: How many children can the scarf go around? Would the scarf be long enough for an animal like a giraffe? This activity could be linked to stories about scarves, such as *The Red Scarf* by Anne Villeneuve (2010) or *The Giraffe in a Scarf (Know How to Grow)* by Karen Clarke (2012).

• Use nursery rhymes or play games such as 'What's the time Mr Wolf?' These allow children to explore the language associated with measures, in this case time.

• *Longest rod*. In this game each child collects a specific colour of bricks that can fit together. A bag is passed around and each child takes a brick. If the brick is of the colour they are collecting, the child adds it to the other bricks they have; if it is not the same colour, they must discard it. The winner of the game is the child who ends up with the longest set of bricks joined together. You may want to limit the number of times the bag goes around the group before you finish and compare the lengths of the brick-rods that the children have made.

• *Give a mouse a tail*. Give each child a mouse and materials for them to make a tail for their mouse. When all the mice have tails, these can be compared and ordered.

• Cooking activities offer children good opportunities for using measures in a real-life context. Such activities can be used to explore ordering, sequencing and the selection of appropriate measures.

• *Shadow hunt*. This activity requires a day and time when shadows are created outdoors. Children can look at shadows created by various objects as well as by their own bodies. They can mark around the shadows, including their own if working in pairs. Discuss with the children how the shadows might be measured. Ask questions about the lengths of the shadows; for example, are the children's shadows shorter or longer than their own bodies?

• *Sequence jigsaw hunt*. Hide pictures around the classroom or outside, whichever is appropriate, and divide the class into teams to find the pictures. The pictures can show events from a well-known story, a sequence of numbers, or the times of events. Tell the children how many pictures are needed to complete the sequence; the first group to complete the task is the winner. You can vary the difficulty level by mixing sequences to be found and by changing the choice of pictures in the sequences. You could extend this activity by having sequences with a missing piece which the children must insert into the sequence to complete the task.

Activities as part of continuous provision

In addition to specifically planned activities, there should be resources available in locations around the setting from which the children can choose, enabling them to explore aspects of measures, including comparison. Since sand and water trays are available in most settings all of the time, here we concentrate on other kinds of activities. To stimulate children's interest, it is worth changing every few days the types of containers available; also offer different types of materials for children to work with, and encourage different ways of using equipment which is around all the time.

- Make a house for a small creature. Provide a small soft toy and materials for building a house for the creature. Each time the activity is provided, change the kinds of materials available for children to work with; this helps them to develop a sense of different measures and finer motor skills.

- Make a tent for a giant. This is similar to the previous activity, but now use a very large soft toy or a giant that the children have already built. Then provide materials for the children to make a tent for the large animal or giant.

- Have a collection of measuring instruments for children to explore in their play. In a school there are likely to be resources around which could be used to start this collection. Children can be encouraged to bring items from home to add to the collection. The collection could include tape measures, cups, spoons, scales and rulers. Provide clipboards, paper and pens for the children to record their ideas as they explore the instruments.

- Have children build towers with bricks or blocks and experiment with how tall these can be built. This is a good activity to set up outdoors. (If using larger, heavier bricks, draw a safety ring around the building area; at any time the child doing the building is the only one within the marked circle, to prevent others from possibly being hurt when the towers collapse.)

- *Matching sizes*. Provide toy creatures in a range of sizes, along with spoons, plates and other equipment of appropriate sizes for the toys. Ask children to match items of the right size for each toy.

- *Ordering masses*. Provide coloured containers of the same size and shape but with differing contents. Ask children to explore the comparative masses of the containers and to place them in order on a track (which has one end labelled lightest and the other end labelled heaviest). The same track (with different labels) could also be used for comparing measures other than mass.

Play environments for children to explore measures

Different kinds of play environments provide children with opportunities to explore specific aspects of mathematics as well as to use mathematical language appropriately and reinforce their skills. As a teacher, you need to be aware of how children might exploit these opportunities for incidental reinforcement of skills such as counting or for learning new ideas that arise naturally in the play context. Although initially you may set up an area for children to explore, it is important that they be able to add to and develop the environment as they play, changing the emphasis according to their needs and interests. The following ideas are meant to provide starting points for creating your own play environments for children to explore key aspects of measures.

Post office

Idea

Set up a play area as a post office. This is a particularly good environment to explore around holidays when gifts are sent out, eg, Christmas with presents or Easter with eggs.

Equipment

Cardboard boxes of different shapes and sizes; a set of scales to weigh parcels; address labels and envelopes; possibly a wheeled cart for delivering parcels and letters; a list of prices of stamps for letters and a list of charges for delivering packages of various sizes.

Outcomes

Children will be heard exploring the language of cost, mass and size. They will have opportunities to compare the sizes and weights of parcels.

The three bears' cottage

Idea

Make an area into a cottage inhabited by the three bears. Reading the story or, better still, different versions of the story would help the children understand the context.

Equipment

Masks for the bears and Goldilocks; three chairs of different sizes; beds, bowls and spoons; a small cooker for pretend porridge.

Outcomes

In recreating the story, children will need to order the bowls, spoons, chairs and beds from largest to smallest.

Baby clinic

Idea

Make an area into a clinic for babies. This activity could be linked to the topic of growth, development and change.

Equipment

Scales for weighing babies; tape measures; paper and pencils for recording the measurements of babies; coats and stethoscopes for the doctors; aprons or uniforms for the nurses. You may also want to include prescription pads for medicines.

Outcomes

This activity could involve measuring length, weight, head circumference and body temperature. There will be opportunities for comparing measurements and mathematical mark making.

Car wash

Idea

Set up a play area as a car wash, to encourage children to think about volume and capacity. In warmer weather this could be an outdoor activity; or it could be done indoors on a small scale in a water tray.

Equipment

Buckets and sponges; cars or bikes to wash; a hose for washing vehicles (if outdoors). You might also include signs for opening and closing hours, and paper and pens for a booking system.

Outcomes

There are opportunities for comparing how many buckets of water it takes to clean different-sized cars and bikes. How much water do different buckets hold?

Pirate ship

Idea

Create a pirate ship with sails, a wheel on the bridge, a compass and any other possible part of a ship, depending on the space and resources available. This can be an indoor or outdoor activity.

Equipment

Planks for walking; mops and buckets for cleaning the deck; string or rope with knots tied at regular intervals; small weight for measuring the depth of water to prevent the ship from running aground; material for sails and flags.

Outcomes

Children will have opportunities to explore the language of measures and comparison, such as 'long enough', 'too short', 'full bucket', 'half full', 'empty'.

Assessing children's skills

Can children:

- use mathematical vocabulary correctly in relation to measures;
- match objects that have similarities with respect to height, length, mass and volume;
- compare the size of objects, referring to the objects' length, mass, height and volume;
- order items from heaviest to lightest, longest to shortest and so on;
- recognise relationships such as 'A is taller than B' and 'X is heavier than Y';
- estimate a range of measures using appropriate standard units?

Test your subject knowledge

Can you answer the following questions?

1. How many grams are there in 5kg?

2. What time is 17:00 by a 12-hour clock?

3. What would be an estimate of the distance between London and Stratford upon Avon?

4. In what units would you measure the mass of a large lorry?

5. American recipes use cup measures. What size is this?

6. How much beer does a German stein hold?

Extend your subject knowledge

Review the following standard units and check that you know which measure each one is used for and its relationship with other units used for the same measure. Place each unit in the appropriate column of the table, and write in any relationships between different units associated with the same measure. A couple of examples are shown.

» gram, pint, square millimetre, mile, metre, tonne, centimetre, litre, square metre, millilitre, foot, ounce, square centimetre, yard, kilogram, gallon, inch, millimetre, pound, kilometre, centilitre

Length	Relationship	Mass/ Weight	Relationship	Capacity	Relationship	Area	Relationship
		gram (g)					
		kilogram (kg)	1 kg = 1000g				
		ounce (oz)	1 ounce = 28.3495g				

Critical learning points from this chapter

» Measures are the most widely used aspect of mathematics.

» Children need to learn the correct usage of vocabulary associated with measures.

» Children need practice in comparing measures.

» Before children can begin to make measurements, they need to know the extent of each measure, ie, where it begins and where it ends.

» Children begin to use appropriate tools for measurement.

» Children begin to understand the use of non-standard and standard units.

» Children need practice in using measures before they can estimate appropriately.

Critical reflection

Observe children playing in a sand and water tray or similar environment, where they are filling and emptying containers. Note how the children keep track of the number of times they use one container to fill another. What do you notice about the children's talk relating to measures? What kinds of questions might you ask to extend their learning? How might you use your observations to plan the next steps for the children's learning? How would you guide the children to move from non-standard to standard units in this context?

Try one of the Piagetian conservation tasks with a group of children. What kinds of responses do you get? How might you use this information to assess their skills and plan the next steps in their learning?

Consider how measures are used by children and adults in the setting/school and how the connections between these activities and the mathematics of measures are made explicit.

Taking it further

Ainley, J (1991) Is There Any Mathematics in Measurement? in Pimm, D and Love, E (eds) *Teaching and Learning School Mathematics*, pp 69–76. London: Hodder & Stoughton.

>   This chapter explores the relationship between measurement and mathematics.

Haylock, D and Cockburn, A (2008) *Understanding Mathematics for Young Children*. London: Sage.

>   In particular, chapter 7 focuses on measures.

Montague-Smith, A and Price, A (2012) *Mathematics in the Early Years Education* (third edition). London: David Fulton.

>   In particular, chapter 6 focuses on measures.

References

Boulton-Lewis, G M, Wilss, L A and Mutch, S L (1996) An Analysis of Young Children's Strategies and Use of Devices in Length Measurement. *Journal of Mathematical Behavior,* 15: 329–47.

Clarke, K (2012) *The Giraffe in a Scarf (Know How to Grow)*. Norfolk: Bear Tails.

Flavell, J M, Miller, P H and Miller, S A (1993) *Cognitive Development* (third edition). Englewood Cliffs, New Jersey: Prentice-Hall.

Nunes, T, Light, P and Mason, J (1993) Tools for Thought: The Measurement of Length and Area. *Learning and Instruction*, 3(1): 39–54.

Villeneuve, A (2010) *The Red Scarf*. New York: Tundra Books.

5 What will happen if...?

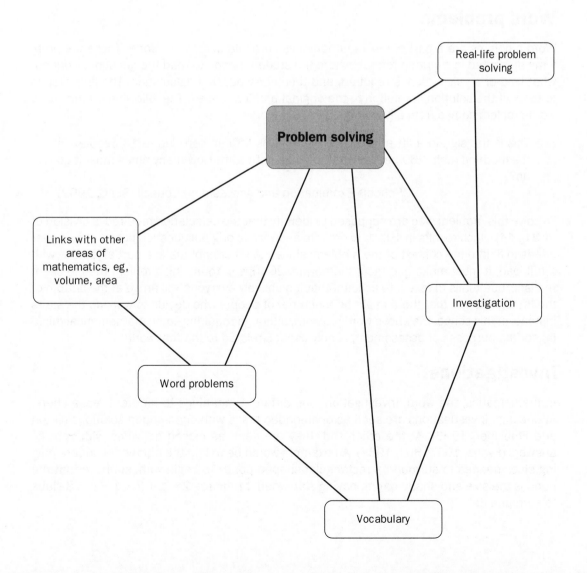

Real-life problem solving

Problem solving

Links with other areas of mathematics, eg, volume, area

Investigation

Word problems

Vocabulary

Introduction

Young children are naturally curious and want to find out about their environment and how things work. Piaget (1963) suggested that children understand only what they discover or invent themselves. They may be observed exploring how to use informal measurement to compare objects, and how to use construction materials to make buildings or other structures; they may be heard posing their own questions about the world around them and then seen working independently or seeking help from others to answer these questions. The term 'problem solving' is often used without definition, and therefore assumptions are frequently made about what it means. One of the issues about this aspect of mathematics is that it lacks a clear definition which encompasses all of the activities typically conducted under this umbrella term. There are a number of areas associated with problem solving that are worth exploring further. This chapter looks at problem solving – what it is, what it is not, and how it helps children to use and apply mathematical knowledge and skills.

Word problems

Word problems are a part of most mathematics curricula across the world. These are problems presented in a written format, where the student needs to read the question, work out what kind of a calculation is required, and then carry out that calculation. The final step is to test out the solution in relation to the original problem posed. The following example of a word problem comes from a Key Stage 3 SATS paper:

> This is the sign in a lift at an office block: 'This lift can carry up to 14 people'. In the morning rush, 269 people want to go up in this lift. How many times must it go up?
>
> Schools Examination and Assessment Council (SEAC, 1992)

To solve this problem, you are supposed to identify that the calculation required is division of 269 by 14, which results in 19.21. In order to answer the original question posed, the answer needs to fit into the context of the problem; since the lift cannot make a partial journey with a full load, it must make one more journey, ie, 20 trips in total. This problem tries to seem realistic, but it fails to take into account that it's unlikely everyone will arrive at the bottom of the lift together, or that there might be a number of people who decide to walk up the stairs instead. In this sense, the above word problem, although requiring some mathematical thinking for the purposes of assessment, is only pseudo-related to the real world.

Investigations

In mathematics, the word 'investigation' has different meanings to different researchers. At one end, investigations are seen as open-ended tasks with open-ended solutions (Orton and Frobisher, 1996). At the other end, they are seen as closed activities with specific answers (Evans, 1987; HMI, 1985). An example would be to find the number of square paving slabs needed to surround a rectangular-shaped pond. To begin with, suppose that the pond is the size and shape of one paving slab; then it requires $2 \times 1 + 2 \times 1 + 4 = 8$ slabs to surround it:

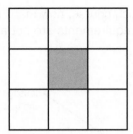

Starting from this simplest case, other cases can be investigated; for example, if the pond is the size and shape of four paving slabs, then how many slabs are needed around it? This kind of problem has a specific answer that can be distilled into an algebraic expression:

number of slabs required = 2 × length of one side + 2 × length of second side + 4

(where 'length' is measured by number of paving slabs).

This type of extending-the-pattern investigation can be completed in various ways. Most often, we look at each item in the sequence and work out how it is used to form the next one; that is, we find out how two successive items depend upon each other. Once we know the relationship between successive items in the sequence, it is easy to continue the pattern and find one item after another. However, this requires us to look at each item in turn, and can be a laborious process. The next step is to move from following such a pattern term by term along a sequence to deducing a general statement that will allow you to find any item in the sequence without necessarily knowing the previous one. This is where algebraic expressions can help, as they assist in moving the investigator from specific cases to a generalised statement about the problem. Algebra is not an expectation of the curriculum in the Early Years, but the thinking processes that go on before using algebra can be developed in young learners. It is also important for adults to know where this learning leads.

Another example of a 'closed' type of investigation is a 'combinatorics' problem, where permutations and combinations of a finite number of options are considered. Imagine a menu like the one below:

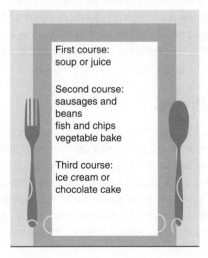

First course:
soup or juice

Second course:
sausages and
beans
fish and chips
vegetable bake

Third course:
ice cream or
chocolate cake

If you must choose one item for each course, how many possible meals can be eaten from this menu, assuming that dietary requirements are not an issue? The choices can be illustrated using a tree diagram:

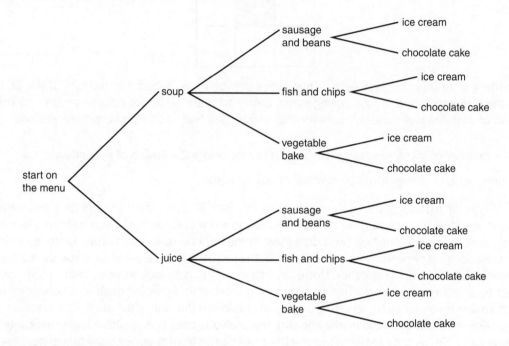

This shows that there are 12 possible options.

Problem solving

Problem solving should allow children to make use of the knowledge and skills they have learnt in other contexts to assist them in solving problems. This characterisation of problem solving was at the heart of the introduction of the 'using and applying' attainment target in the National Curriculum documentation in the UK. Hiebert et al (1997) state that tasks that promote understanding *are ones for which students have no memorised rules, nor for which they perceive there is one right solution method. Rather, the tasks are viewed as opportunities to explore mathematics and come up with reasonable methods for solution* (Hiebert et al, 1997, page 8).

Real-life problem solving

Real-life problem solving sounds straightforward, but it can present many difficulties as real-life problems don't always have a solution and can involve 'messy' data. This is often the label given to word problems set in a 'real-life' context, such as those that involve travel, baking or similar activities; but does providing such a context make this kind of problem actually related to real life, or is it just another example of a pseudo-practical problem? Real-life problems should arise from the children's interests and be problems that they actually want to solve, which are not necessarily problems that adults have decided are important.

Critical question

» *Read the following problem and decide whether or not you think it is a real-life problem.*

A child wants to make six cakes. If they know that 3kg of flour is enough for 24 cakes, how much flour will they need?

Comment

At one level, this is a real-life practical problem, as recipes may give quantities of ingredients for an amount different than you might wish to make. The problem is phrased in a word problem format and could be solved in a number of ways; the most common method is to find the amount of flour needed for one cake and then multiply this by 6 to get the final answer: 3kg is 3000g, so each cake requires 3000 ÷ 24 = 125g of flour; hence 6 cakes require 125g × 6 = 750g. The problem could provide interest to the children, but the context is actually irrelevant to the calculation required.

How to choose appropriate problem-solving activities for children

Goffin and Tull (1985) identified four key questions to assist adults in selecting appropriate problem-solving activities for young children:

1. Is the problem going to be meaningful and interesting to the children?

2. Can the problem be solved at a variety of levels?

3. Is there a rationale for the solution and why it needs to be found?

4. Can the actions taken to solve the problem be evaluated?

In addition to these key questions, there are general questions that can be used to judge what makes a good activity. The following are two lists of such questions (Briggs, 2009). They can be used generally to make decisions in choosing tasks for children to work on, whether these are problem-solving tasks or not.

Does the intended task allow:

• access for all;

• possibility for extension;

• possibility for narrowing or simplifying;

• enjoyment?

Does it offer/present:

• a practical starting point;

• stimuli and opportunities for mathematical discussion;

• opportunities and reasons for children to work and talk together;

- reasons for children to record their ideas;

- clarity of underlying mathematics;

- opportunities for repetition without becoming meaningless – both for teachers and for children?

Critical question

» *Find three or four problem-solving activities and check them against the two lists above. Do these activities meet all the requirements? If not, where do they fail to match the expectations? Would they still be suitable activities in another situation, and when would it be appropriate to use them?*

Specific adult-led activities associated with problem solving

The following are activities that an adult can plan and prepare for a small group of children to familiarise them with mathematical problem solving through exploration and talk. Although these are adult-led activities, they don't have to be formally structured; rather than adhering rigidly to your initial plans, let the children's interest guide the activities.

- Set children the problem of building a set of stairs that a teddy can climb to get to an item currently out of reach. Children can be asked to draw their stair designs on small whiteboards before selecting appropriate materials and starting to build. It is useful to evaluate different designs and builds, focusing on the positive aspects of all sets of stairs. Can the children build a sequence of stairs to reach different heights?

- *Snowmen.* This is a 'combinatorics' problem and requires a large snowman and various brooms, hats and scarves in order to make different combinations. Ask children to make as many different snowmen as possible by choosing a broom, hat and scarf in different combinations. To record the different snowmen, children could be given sheets with blank snowmen drawn on them.

Discuss what is different and the same about the snowmen children have made, and check for unique snowmen.

- *River crossing.* This is an old problem which emphasises logical thinking. A man arrives at a river and wants to cross. He has with him a goat, a wolf and a cabbage. He finds a boat but it can only hold the man and one other item. He needs to get everything safely across to the other side of the river. But if he leaves the goat with the wolf, the wolf will eat the goat; if he leaves the goat and the cabbage together, the goat will eat the cabbage. Ask the children to work out how the man can complete the task. Children might suggest that the man can throw the cabbage across, or that one of the animals can swim across, so it is worth thinking through the possible responses. Assuming a very wide and fast-flowing river is a good way to circumvent this issue. Puppets and a toy boat can help children to work out solutions by physically moving the items from one side of the river to the other.

- *Moving the hat.* The diagram below represents eight children (the circles) standing in a three-by-three grid.

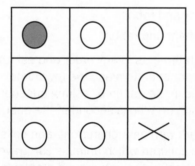

The person wearing a hat (the shaded circle) has to move to the empty square marked with a cross. To get there they can only move into an empty square in front of, to either side or behind them, but they cannot move diagonally. These same moves are the only ones allowed for everybody else. What is the smallest number of moves needed so that the person with the hat can get from their starting position to the one marked with a cross?

- If the previous problem was changed to a four-by-four grid with one empty square, what would be the smallest number of moves? What if the square grid were even bigger? Is there a pattern? Can you tell how many moves are needed for any square grid? This problem is similar to the sliding squares puzzles that are often found in Christmas crackers.

- *Bikes in the shed.* Suppose that a child owns five bikes and a large shed. If they can see two bikes outside the shed, how many are inside? How many different ways can the bikes be arranged inside and outside the shed? You can change the problem by increasing the numbers of bikes and sheds for children to investigate further.

- *The milk crate problem.* A milk crate is six holes wide by four holes deep, ie, it has 24 spaces for bottles. If a suitable plastic crate is available, then that would work most effectively for this activity, but you could also draw the crate as a grid on paper. The children are given 18 milk bottles, or skittles to stand on the paper. The bottles must be placed in the crate so that there is an even number of bottles in every row and column. The children can work together to check each of the views. This is a problem that children can play with and invent their own rules for after they have been guided by an adult.

- *Filling containers*. This is a practical problem that starts with finding as many things as possible to fit into a matchbox or similar-sized container. The children can discuss the strategies they use to find things that are small enough to fit. From this you can move on to looking at different kinds of containers and how they might be filled without any gaps. This problem links to volume and capacity.

- *Bus stop queue*. Make or place a bus stop sign in the middle of the group and ask children to place toy animals in order in the queue by reading statements such as:

  Teddy is at the end of the queue.

  Rabbit is in the middle of the queue.

  Elephant is nearest the bus stop.

  Giraffe is between teddy and rabbit.

  Snake is between elephant and rabbit.

  You can read out the statements in any order and ask the children at each stage if they have enough information to place the toy animals in the queue. Discuss the positions of the animals in the queue by asking questions like 'Is the end of the queue the same as last?' or 'Who is second in the queue?'

- *Who will fit?* Make an ark with an arch in front, and collect a range of toy animals of different sizes. Ask the children which animals can travel on the ark if they have to fit through the arch. (Children often think around problems, so you may have children saying that animals can walk around the arch to get on the ark.) Once children have been introduced to the initial idea, they can play with other rules about which animals can travel on the ark. For example, you could specify how many legs are allowed on board the ark for any one journey.

- *Party or picnic planner*. Have children help plan a party or picnic that is to be held in the setting. This is a good opportunity to practise collecting data with a purpose. For example, children's dietary requirements and food preferences will have to be taken into account, and the children will need to find out how much drink a bottle of squash will make so that they can estimate the number of bottles needed for the class as a whole.

- Games like 'connect 4' or 'noughts and crosses' can be used to introduce strategic thinking and tactics. Is it better to start first or second? With noughts and crosses, is there a first mark and position that is helpful for winning? These kinds of games can be played on a table top or on a larger scale outdoors.

Activities as part of continuous provision

In addition to specifically planned activities, there should be resources available in locations around the setting from which the children can choose, enabling them to explore solving different kinds of problems.

- *Span the gap*. Have spaces available where there are opportunities to safely create bridge-like structures. This allows children to engage in problem solving as part of their play without setting up specific activities.

- *Stepping stones*. Allow children to create pathways across a marked-off area with representations of stepping stones. Again, there doesn't need to be a formal activity associated with the equipment.

- *Pattern making*. Provide a box of pattern-making equipment which children can use to create their own repeating and unique patterns. This helps to develop their mathematical thinking. The collection might include matchsticks, buttons, counters, and other similar objects. Adults observing could ask questions like the following as prompts: 'What comes next in your pattern?' 'What pattern are you making?' 'Tell me about the pattern you have made.' 'If I wanted to add the next piece, how would I know which item to choose?'

- *Large building blocks*. These can be an effective stimulus for problem-solving activities associated with building structures and understanding shape, space and position. Children can explore symmetry and think about how to make entrances and windows for structures.

- Computer games or games on handheld electronic devices can help children learn to solve problems in different situations and for different reasons. Can I collect all the fruit to feed an animal? How do I progress to the next level of the game? Playing such games involves problem-solving skills.

- Board games for children can help them to learn about turn taking and other rules of the game as well as to gain skills in logical thinking and strategy development. Such games could form part of a bank of resources that children could borrow to take home and play with adults or other children, linking activities in the setting with activities that may go on at home.

Play environments for children to explore problem solving

Different kinds of play environments provide children with opportunities to explore specific aspects of mathematics as well as to use mathematical language appropriately and reinforce their skills. As a teacher, you need to be aware of how children might exploit these opportunities for incidental reinforcement of skills such as counting or for learning new ideas that arise naturally in the play context. Although initially you may set up an area for children to explore, it is important that they be able to add to and develop the environment as they play, changing the emphasis according to their needs and interests. The following ideas are meant to provide starting points for creating your own play environments.

Buried treasure

Idea

In this activity children find items on a list and then sort them. The items can relate to a current topic or theme in the setting/school. Children have to solve the problem of finding all the items on the list and then sorting and checking that they have found everything.

Equipment

A large pit or tray; a variety of items of different sizes to hide in the sand and under or behind pots and other containers placed in the sand; a list of the items to be recovered from the sand, possibly with pictures, which the children can use to check that they have everything. Make sure there are more items hidden than listed so that the activity is not just about collecting everything in the sand.

Outcomes

Children will work systematically with perseverance to collect the items. They will count the items, sort them appropriately, and check them against the list to make sure they have everything required.

Mazes

Idea

Have children design and plan a maze, giving instructions for the route to the middle of the maze.

Equipment

So that children understand what a maze actually is, show them pictures of mazes, or make available short screen games that allow children to experience solving the route to the middle of a maze; alternatively, it may be possible to take the children on a trip to a real maze. Provide paper and pens for the maze-designing phase, and large empty boxes or building blocks to use for building the maze.

Outcomes

Children will draw their designs and, with appropriate assistance, build a maze. Further, with adult support, they can use directional language to plan the route for others to follow to the middle of the maze.

Cinderella or Cinderfella and the slipper

Idea

Children select a slipper and decide how they will test its size against each child in the class to find out who is Cinderella or Cinderfella for the day. You can have a rule that the slipper is not allowed to leave the display case/stand or its vicinity, so children have to find a way of determining how big the slipper is in order to measure it against all the feet in the class. If more than one child has the same foot size, the children need to decide how they are going to choose just one Cinderella or Cinderfella. A different-sized slipper can be used each time this game is played.

Equipment

A collection of slippers of different sizes; tape measures and other measuring devices; squared and plain paper to draw on; clipboards and pens/pencils to record names and whether or not each child's foot has been measured.

Outcomes

Children may draw around the slipper on paper or make measurements against which they can compare foot size. They will keep track of their efforts to find the Cinderella or Cinderfella. The officials working on this problem will need to cooperate and decide how they will organise their work and carry it out. They will, with adult guidance, review how successful their problem solving has been.

Cracking the code

Idea

The goal is for children to crack the code to a combination lock; they gain prizes by solving clues that lead to the correct number.

Equipment

Combination locks which can be set and opened only with the correct number combination; several sets of prepared clues leading to different answers so that several groups of children can play in this environment; small prizes; paper and pens for any recording or calculations that might be needed. For example, if you use a combination lock with four numbers, you could give clues such as: 'the first is the number that appears at the bottom of the clock' (6), 'the second is the number of plants in the room' (7), 'the third is on their own' (1), 'the last is nothing at all' (0). Clues should be tailored to the age and ability range of the children.

Outcomes

Children will collaborate to solve the clues. They will apply their knowledge and skills to count, calculate, measure or observe, depending on the clues provided.

FOCUS ON RESEARCH

Polya and beyond

George Polya (1887–1985) was probably the first person to explore problem solving from a mathematical perspective. He proposed a rubric or set of rules to guide the problem solver (adapted from Polya, 1957):

1.   Understand the problem – identify what information is given, the scope of the problem, whether a solution is possible and, if so, under what conditions.

2.   Devise a plan – determine what further information might be needed and how this could be collected, what resources are needed, whether similar problems have been solved and could yield helpful information, and whether the problem could be restated in a different way that would be more helpful for finding a solution.

3.   Carry out the plan – collect appropriate information and resources and carry out the steps towards a solution, checking each step as it is completed.

4.   Review or extend the solution – examine the solution obtained and think about whether it answers the original question posed, whether the solution is reasonable, whether a solution could be obtained in a different way, and whether the solution to this problem might be used to solve other problems.

Although this work is somewhat dated, current research still tends to focus on the issue of teaching general problem-solving strategies like the rubric above, as opposed to teaching skills within particular areas of problem solving. De Groot (1965) provided an alternative view of problem solving through his research into chess players, who can learn the moves quickly but take much longer to reach master level. In order to become an expert problem solver, knowledge needs to be developed within the specific domain (De Groot, 1965; Sweller and Cooper, 1985). This can happen only through opportunities for the individual to engage with a large number of problem-solving strategies relevant to a particular area. Just knowing general problem-solving strategies will not make learners expert problem solvers, and this is at the heart of the difficulties inherent in many problem-solving activities presented in books for adults working with children. It is important for teachers to look critically at the activities and strategies suggested that are labelled as problem solving.

What can support children's mathematical problem solving – especially in relation to word problems – is to encourage children to use drawing to help visualise the specific problems to be solved. Csíkos et al (2012) have experimented with this approach in Hungary. They found that in order to move away from drill-and-practice arithmetic tasks 'dressed up' as word problems towards in-depth problem solving, children need to develop visualisation skills by using drawing to assist them. This view of 'visual imagery', which comes from Presmag (1986), is as a mental scheme for representing information or an object when it is not actually present. Jonassen (2003) supports this view, saying that *successful problem solving requires the comprehension of relevant textual information, the capacity to visualize the data* (Jonassen, 2003, page 269).

Critical question

»   *Try two similar problem-solving activities with children – one where the children are encouraged to use pictorial representations of the problem to assist them with obtaining a solution, and one where they must visualise the problem mentally. Observe the differences in responses of children in the group.*

Comment

Often whole groups of children are taught a single strategy, regardless of whether or not it is the most appropriate for all learners. Although Early Years education has a tradition of working with children as individuals, there is still a tendency to employ similar approaches with the majority of learners. You may well have observed that some children found it easier to engage with the problem when asked to draw a picture, whereas other children found this to be a barrier to their thinking. It is worth considering why children have different responses to using drawing. Is it that some children just don't like to draw? Are these the children who can already visualise problems in their head? If they are in this category, you might think about providing extension activities to develop their skills further. Are there children in the group who spent more time on the drawing and little on actually solving the problem? These children may need different types of problems to engage their mathematical thinking or additional support to assist them to get started with mathematical problem solving.

Working with the child's own interests

Young children can pose themselves and others interesting questions to explore. For example, when reading about historical lives, they will encounter living conditions different from their own. Working out the living space of a Victorian slum family can enhance their understanding of shape and space as well as their appreciation of changes in the lives of children. Drawing on the floor or playground the space for a large Victorian family to live in and walking around that space or finding out how the family would have slept in the space can address children's initial curiosity and also stimulate further questions. Children set and solve their own problems in the course of play on a regular basis; you are more likely to see this going on through careful observation of the patterns of their play, especially in open spaces out of doors. You might overhear the following starts to conversations when children are in problem-solving mode: 'I think...', 'I can try...', 'We could try...', 'What will happen if...', 'If...'. You are likely to see children building structures that will allow them to form dens, bridges across gaps, paths or roadways. You may also observe children choosing appropriate tools based upon function and purpose, such as a box that can fit a particular number of toys to act as a bus or shed. Although observation and listening will give you access to some aspects of children's problem-solving processes, asking children what are they thinking can help you gain additional insights into the processes they are undertaking. Such questioning needs to be done carefully so that it does not interrupt the flow of children's play but, rather, adds to the reflections the children are making.

Critical question

» *Observe children's play both indoors and outdoors to see which situations children like to use as the basis of problem solving for themselves. What kinds of questions do they ask themselves or the others with whom they are playing? Do they ask these questions expecting answers or not? How could these processes be supported further with resources or sensitive and appropriate adult support?*

Assessing children's skills

Can children:

- understand the problem to be solved;

- plan a solution;

- work out a solution;

- reflect on ways of working;

- use appropriate mathematical language to talk about the process of problem solving;

- use appropriate language to explain and justify their ideas;

- model problems appropriately using available resources;

- use drawings where appropriate to support their thinking?

Test your subject knowledge

Try to answer the following questions.

1. Growing crosses – can you work out the pattern in this sequence of crosses? (The first two are shown below.) How many squares would there be in the fifth cross, the tenth cross, the nth cross? Try to find algebraic expressions for all these cases.

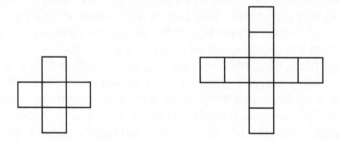

2. A football team wants a new strip. The shorts, top and socks must each be in one of the three colours red, white and blue. How many possible team strips can there be?

3. Can you extend the following pattern? Reflect on how you are working on this. What do you focus your attention on in order to solve the problem? What is the 35th object in this pattern? Can you also find an algebraic solution?

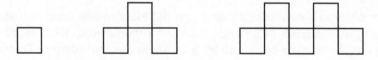

4. Try one of the Japanese puzzles such as Kakura or Sudoku to extend your thinking about mathematical puzzles and to exercise the brain.

Extend your subject knowledge

» Explore a problem or an investigation with your colleagues and discuss how you approached the task. What issues arose in tackling the problem? Did you find it helpful to draw or model the problem with equipment? Did you all tackle the task in the same way? What was the source of any differences? What have you learnt from doing this task that would be helpful in planning and supporting children to work on appropriate problems?

» Find a pattern or sequence that you can explore with the children; it could be one from this chapter or other resources. Challenge yourself to try something with the children that you have not explored beforehand so that you are learning alongside the children.

» Find out about games from other countries or historical games that could be explored in the class.

» Build up a bank of activities that the children can choose to engage with as part of the continuous provision in the setting.

Critical learning points from this chapter

» Children naturally solve problems in the course of their play.

» There are a number of different contexts for problem solving, including word problems, investigations and real-life problems.

» Problem solving allows children to use and apply their mathematical knowledge.

» Problem-solving activities can help young children develop their visualisation skills.

» Problem-solving skills and knowledge can help young children develop algebraic thinking.

» When problem solving, there will be times that the outcomes may not be certain; but the process is the important aspect of problem solving, especially when related to real life.

Critical reflection

Review the opportunities that exist in the setting for children to explore problems mathematically and the frequency of their availability. Try a pattern investigation with children and observe how they work on the task. Observe children's free play to see how much problem solving occurs naturally, and consider how additional or different resources might facilitate this further. Listen and observe carefully to see if children raise their own problems that could be solved in the setting and be a vehicle for exploring mathematical thinking.

Taking it further

Goffin, S and Tull, C (1985) Problem Solving: Encouraging Active Learning. *Young Children*, 40: 28–32.

> This article provides a good starting point for thinking about the process of active learning in relation to problem solving.

Haylock, D and Cockburn, A (2008) *Understanding Mathematics for Young Children*. London: Sage.

> In particular, chapter 10 focuses on using and applying mathematics.

Montague-Smith, A and Price, A (2012) *Mathematics in the Early Years Education* (third edition). London: David Fulton.

> In particular, chapter 3 discusses the elements of problem solving with number.

References

Briggs, M (2009) Listening Matters, in Housartt, J and Mason, J (eds) *Listening Counts: Listening to Young Learners of Mathematics*. London: Trentham Books.

Csíkos, C, Szitányi, J and Kelemen, R (2012) The Effects of Using Drawings in Developing Young Children's Mathematical Word Problem Solving: A Design Experiment with Third-grade Hungarian Students. *Educational Studies in Mathematics*, 81(1): 47–65.

De Groot, A (1965) *Thought and Choice in Chess*. The Hague, The Netherlands: Mouton.

Evans, J (1987) Investigations: The State of the Art. *Mathematics in School*, 16(1): 27–30.

Goffin, S and Tull, C (1985) Problem Solving: Encouraging Active Learning. *Young Children*, 40: 28–32.

Hiebert, J, Carpenter, T P, Fennema, E, Fuson, K, Wearne, D, Murray, H, Olivier, A and Human, P (1997) *Making Sense: Teaching and Learning Mathematics with Understanding*. Portsmouth, New Hampshire: Heinemann.

HMI (1985) *Mathematics from 5 to 16*. London: Her Majesty's Stationery Office (HMSO).

Jonassen, D H (2003) Designing Research-based Instruction for Story Problems. *Educational Psychology Review*, 15: 267–96.

Orton, A and Frobisher, L (1996) *Insights into Teaching Mathematics*. London: Cassell.

Paiget, J (1963) *The Origins of Intelligence in Children*. New York: WW Norton.

Polya, G (1957) *How to Solve It* (second edition). Princeton, New Jersey: Princeton University Press.

Presmag, N (1986) Visualisation in High School Mathematics. *For the Learning of Mathematics*, 6: 42–46.

Schools Examination and Assessment Council (SEAC) (1992) *Mathematics Tests 1992*. London: SEAC/University of London.

Sweller, J and Cooper, G (1985) The Use of Worked Examples as a Substitute for Problem Solving in Learning Algebra. *Cognition and Instruction*, 2: 59–89.

6 Who has the most?

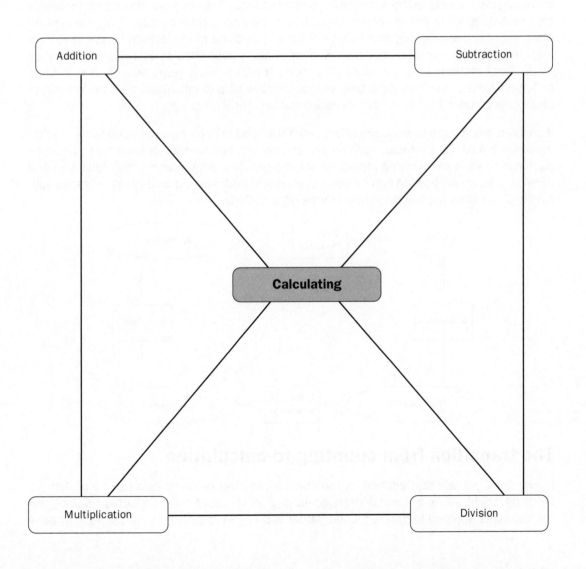

Introduction

Understanding of place value, fluency in mental methods, and good recall of number facts such as multiplication tables and number bonds are considered by the schools to be essential precursors for learning traditional vertical algorithms (methods) for addition, subtraction, multiplication and division.

(Ofsted, 2011, page 6)

This chapter looks at extending the counting and calculating begun in chapter 2, developing the processes into the four rules of arithmetic: addition, subtraction, multiplication and division. The rules of arithmetic are often taught separately, but it is important that children understand the relationships between them so that they can develop flexible strategies for calculation, a prerequisite to becoming successful mathematicians. Rather than focus on written calculations, here we emphasise having children work with concrete equipment and mental methods to develop their ability to visualise numbers and move from the concrete to the abstract. Adults in the setting can model the recording of calculations, and children's own recording, while not expected, should be encouraged (see chapter 2 for elementary mathematical mark making and chapter 8 for a discussion of the different ways of recording). The development of a child's calculating skills is supported by knowing the everyday language of mathematics; therefore an important part of early years education is to build children's skills in mathematical talk, so that they are able to talk about their exploration of ideas (see chapter 7 for more details about mathematical language).

If children are to learn to calculate effectively, they need to know how the operations of arithmetic are linked. For example, addition and subtraction are inverses of each other, because each can be seen as reversing the action of the other. The same is true of multiplication and division. Also, multiplication can be seen as repeated addition and division as repeated subtraction. The following diagram shows these relationships.

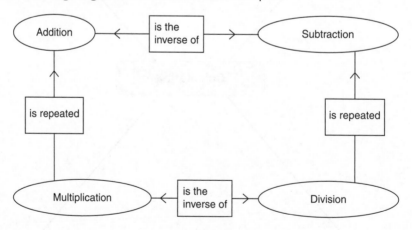

The transition from counting to calculation

In chapter 2 we saw that addition of the numbers of objects in two sets can be performed by using 'count all' as the initial strategy, moving on to 'count on' from either number and then towards applying known facts. *Altogether* is a key word to use in the teaching of early addition, as it emphasises the combining of two or more groups of objects; for example, when counting two groups of items, you would ask the children, 'How many do we have *altogether*?'

A similar process occurs in subtraction. The first strategy is usually to compare the quantities of two groups using one-to-one correspondence, in order to find the difference. The next stage is to count on or back from one of the quantities, to find how many more or fewer the other group has. Counting back from a fixed number when taking away is the equivalent of the counting on strategy in addition.

Partitioning numbers and collecting known facts

Numbers, even small ones, can be partitioned, and this strategy helps children to under-stand and memorise known facts. If we take a number, say 6, it can be partitioned in the following ways:

$$0 + 6 = 6$$
$$1 + 5 = 6$$
$$2 + 4 = 6$$
$$3 + 3 = 6$$
$$4 + 2 = 6$$
$$5 + 1 = 6$$
$$6 + 0 = 6$$

Partitioning can be done with any positive whole number, and you can have children make books of the numbers and the number-sentence patterns created by partitioning. Groups of objects representing different combinations of numbers could be left out for children to find and place with their number-bond patterns. The aim of such activities is to guide children in making the shift from 'count all' to 'counting on' and then towards establishing known facts.

Similarly, patterns for subtraction can be formed:

$$6 - 0 = 6$$
$$6 - 1 = 5$$
$$6 - 2 = 4$$
$$6 - 3 = 3$$
$$6 - 4 = 2$$
$$6 - 5 = 1$$
$$6 - 6 = 0$$

Discuss with children the patterns created – what do they notice about 6 − 2 = 4 and 6 − 4 = 2? Again, the goal is to move from comparing to counting back and then towards establishing known facts that children can use later in their mathematics learning.

Subtraction

Subtraction is usually seen as 'taking away', and is easy for children to model with equipment. For example, 8 − 4 = 4 can be modelled as follows:

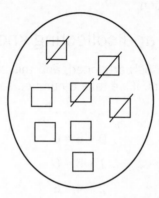

Subtraction can also be seen as finding the difference between quantities; for example, the difference between 4 and 7 is 3. This viewpoint is more challenging for young children, as they tend to focus on physical differences. It is possible to take advantage of this visual focus by making towers of interlocking bricks so that children can directly compare the heights and hence identify the difference between the numbers of bricks.

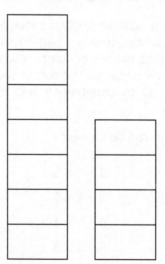

Division and multiplication

The division process is acquired by children mainly through sharing objects equally and then counting how many there are in each group. Many activities in the daily routines of nurseries and Early Years settings involve children sharing food or resources, and children are keen to know that things are shared fairly. They quickly grasp the concept of equality, particularly when it applies to them. So children are most likely to interpret 15 ÷ 3 as sharing 15 items equally between three people. The 15 items would be arranged in three groups:

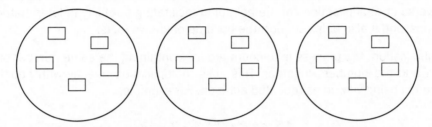

The answer to the sharing question is then the number of items in each group (5). But the same calculation 15 ÷ 3 can also be read as 'How many threes are there in 15?' To answer the question from this viewpoint, the items are grouped in threes and the answer is the total number of groups:

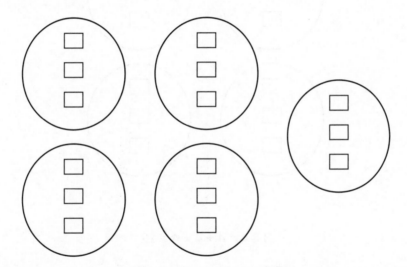

The division process can also be completed by repeated subtraction. In the example of 15 ÷ 3, we take away groups of 3 from 15 until there are no more left:

15 − 3 =	12			
	12 − 3 =	9		
		9 − 3 =	6	
			6 − 3 =	3
				3 − 3 = 0

Then we count up the number of groups of three taken away, which is 5. This procedure also demonstrates a very simple form of 'chunking', which is used as a method of long division later on in primary schools.

When working with division, it is important for young children to understand the two different meanings – equal sharing and repeated subtraction. Equal sharing is the meaning they will encounter most frequently in practical situations, whereas repeated subtraction enables children to see that division is the inverse operation to multiplication. Knowing that division is the inverse of multiplication can be helpful in facilitating flexibility in later mathematical calculations, and it also helps support the build-up of known facts.

With multiplication, the process is to count groups containing the same number of objects and then add the numbers together. This links multiplication directly with addition, with multiplication being viewed as repeated addition. For example,

$$4 \times 3 = 3 + 3 + 3 + 3 = 12$$

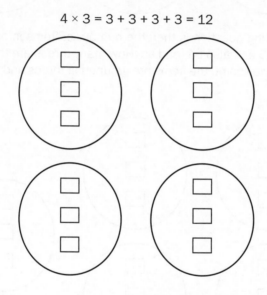

Similarly,

$$3 \times 4 = 4 + 4 + 4 = 12$$

Notice that 4 × 3 = 3 × 4. This illustrates the commutative principle of multiplication first introduced in chapter 2. It is good to help children make explicit links between counting and multiplication; for example, counting in twos gives the two times table. Although young children don't need to be learning times tables explicitly, if they are guided to make connections between different mathematical activities, they can see that they are already building up their multiplication knowledge without even being aware of it, and this will help them gain confidence rather than being worried about learning tables later on. Parents often see times tables as a benchmark for success in mathematics, so explaining the links between counting in different jumps and the times tables can be helpful for both children and parents in understanding the connections between activities and the acquisition of mathematical knowledge.

The importance of place value

Our number system uses place value to allow digits to carry a different value depending upon their position; so 1 on its own has a value of one unit, or simply one, but when placed in a different position, say 1000, the '1' has a value of one thousand. Children need to understand this system and the idea of using zero (0) as a place-holder; for example, 101 has a place-holder in the tens position, so the value of 101 is one hundred and one, with no tens. One of the difficulties children may have with place value stems from the difference between how a number is read and how it is written – for example, if 'one hundred and twenty-six' is written as it is read, we would have 10026; however, the place value system tells us to write digits in specific places indicating whether they represent units, tens or hundreds, so we should write 126. In the Early Years, we do not expect children to be able to record large numbers correctly, but they should be developing their number sense, including an understanding of the place value system.

Millions	Hundred thousands	Ten thousands	Thousands	Hundreds	Tens	Units

Children are often very curious about the counting system and, particularly, the words used to describe large numbers. The following are a few examples of large numbers (in UK terminology) and what they look like in digits. Remember that an American million is the same as a British million, but an American billion is equal to a thousand million while a British billion equals a million million, which is an American trillion.

A million = 1,000,000

A billion = 1,000,000,000,000

A trillion = 1,000,000,000,000,000,000

A quadrillion = 1,000,000,000,000,000,000,000,000,000

Other kinds of numbers

Besides working with whole numbers, young children gain experience of fractions when learning about division. They are not expected to represent fractions using symbols such as ½, but you may observe that they find their own ways to show 'half', as the following example illustrates.

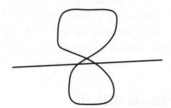

Here the child has clearly understood that a fraction involves an action connected with division, and has therefore represented half of eight as a figure eight with a line through it to show the action of cutting it in half. You may also see children drawing part of a number to show that the whole quantity is not present.

Children also talk about halves in relation to measures, for instance when filling containers. They begin to use 'part', 'a bit' and 'half full' in their vocabulary associated with measures.

Children are likely to encounter decimals in everyday life, for instance when they see money represented, even though money is not a true decimal. They may also come across decimals when playing with a calculator, and they may hear about negative numbers when watching the weather forecast in winter.

Although there is no expectation of young children working with fractions, decimals or negative numbers, these are aspects of mathematics that adults can discuss with children early on. If adults encourage young children to find out more about different kinds of numbers and calculating strategies, the children will feel more confident later on when they are actually expected to work on these areas.

FOCUS ON RESEARCH

Understanding number as a procept

Gray and Tall (1994) defined the term 'procept' as follows:

> An *elementary* procept is the amalgam of three components: a process which produces a mathematical object, and a symbol which is used to represent either process or object. A *procept* consists of a collection of elementary procepts which have the same object.

So the symbol '3' represents not only the *process* of counting 'one, two, three' but also the *concept* of the quantity three. A calculation such as 3 + 4 refers to the process of adding the numbers 3 and 4 together as well as the outcome of doing so, which is the number seven, represented by the symbol 7.

This idea can be quite difficult to grasp, but Gray and Tall's research had a profound effect on the way early arithmetic was viewed from that time onwards. It helped all those working in mathematics education to understand why some children find arithmetic difficult, as they are not able to see and connect these two aspects of number and so persist in working on just the processes involved. For example, such children might continue to use counting strategies for addition, where there are more chances of making an error. On the other hand, children with the flexibility to think about numbers as a 'procept' move more quickly to being able to use known facts and work with a range of strategies adapted to the context of each problem.

Instrumental versus relational understanding

Richard Skemp was a mathematician who also studied psychology and drawing, seeking to use these two disciplines to explain learning in mathematics. His line of argument is based on a Piagetian view of learning and the establishment of schemas which assist in linking what learners already know with new learning. For Skemp, mathematics involves an extensive hierarchy of concepts, and as a consequence learners cannot form any particular concept until they have formed all the subsidiary ones upon which it depends. You could see this as a stage-focused view of mathematical learning. An additional element in Skemp's work is that he viewed emotions as an important part of how we learn mathematics.

In Skemp's seminal work, he suggested that there are two kinds of learning in mathematics:

- Instrumental understanding: this is a mechanistic understanding where rules/methods/procedures are followed, sometimes referred to as 'rote learning'. An important feature of this kind of understanding is that it focuses on what to do, not on why you need to do things.

- Relational understanding: here the focus differs from that of instrumental understanding. In this kind of understanding it is important to know not just how to do things but why and, furthermore, the ways in which different aspects of mathematics connect to each other.

In identifying these two types of understanding, Skemp also made the case that for learners to be successful with mathematics they need both types of understanding.

Critical question

» *Reflect on your own understanding of mathematics in light of Gray and Tall's and Skemp's work. What kind of learner do you think you are? How do you think you were taught to do calculations?*

Comment

You may feel that your own mathematical education experience focused more on instrumental understanding than relational understanding. You may also have reflected that when teaching young children, you emphasise relational understanding more than when you were learning mathematics yourself, especially near exams. Procedures are important to learn, but not without understanding. In mathematics, an 'algorithm' is a step-by-step procedure that produces an answer to a particular problem. You may have been taught to do arithmetic calculations by using algorithms, as these are often seen as the standard or traditional written methods in association with the rules of arithmetic.

Resources for teaching calculation

To support children's early calculating, it is a good idea to offer them a wide variety of resources to assist them in establishing appropriate mental imagery for number work. Offering the same resources for all activities does not allow the children to explore different ways of looking at number. To become successful at mathematics, children need to develop the ability to view number and calculations flexibly.

Number lines and tracks

Number track

1	2	3	4	5	6	7	8	9	10

A number track is a sequence of squares containing the numbers 1, 2, 3, etc. The numbers are inside the squares, like on a game board, and counting is equivalent to moving between the squares. Tracks start at 1, not 0, to ensure that cardinality is linked to ordinality. For example, suppose you are counting up to 4; if the track started at 0, the number 4 would be in the fifth square, so you would need to count five squares to get up to four; if the track starts at 1, the number 4 is in the fourth square, ie, the cardinality matches the ordinality.

Tracks are very useful for doing calculations, particularly for kinaesthetic learners. If the squares are large, a child can physically move along the track, counting on to add (eg, 3 + 4 = 7) or counting back to subtract (eg, 8 − 2 = 6). You can put 0 off the track at one end, so moving off the track means you get zero (eg, 5 − 5 = 0). Children can practise repeated addition (multiplication) by moving up the track in larger jumps of, say, two squares or three squares. The track should go at least as far as 10, preferably further, so that children can see the patterns in counting and calculations more clearly.

Number line

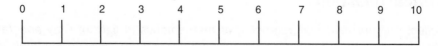

A number line differs from a number track in that the numbers on a number line are on the marks rather than in the spaces between the marks as on a number track. This is an important difference, because it means that calculating involves different moves on a number line and on a number track. On a track, we jump between squares (ie, from one space to another), whereas on a number line we move from mark to mark. Number lines usually start at 0, and even in the Early Years the line should go up to 10 if not beyond. Familiarising young children with this representation of number helps them later on when they are introduced to two other forms of number line: the unnumbered line and the empty number line. Children need to establish a good mental image of a numbered line before they can use the blank forms to assist them with calculations. Both number tracks and number lines represent the continuous nature of number, so children familiar with them will learn not to see numbers in isolation.

Strings of beads

Strings of 30 beads, with each block of ten being the same colour, can be a good resource for counting and calculating. The beads need room to move along the string, and children can physically partition the beads on the string to aid them in counting on and back. The ends of the string should be knotted or secured so that the beads won't get spilt all over the floor. There are commercial versions available, but you could also make your own to suit the needs of individual learners. Children are generally very tactile and like to play with strings of beads, so these can be made part of the continuous provision.

Number squares

Most settings don't have sufficient space to place a 1–100 number line or track in one continuous strip along a wall or floor, in which case number squares can be a compact way of displaying the numbers from 1 to 100.

1	2	3	4	5	6	7	8	9	10
11	12	13	14	15	16	17	18	19	20
21	22	23	24	25	26	27	28	29	30
31	32	33	34	35	36	37	38	39	40
41	42	43	44	45	46	47	48	49	50
51	52	53	54	55	56	57	58	59	60
61	62	63	64	65	66	67	68	69	70
71	72	73	74	75	76	77	78	79	80
81	82	83	84	85	86	87	88	89	90
91	92	93	94	95	96	97	98	99	100

Children might look for the number of their house on the square, or find parts of that number if it is larger than 100; they could find numbers with both digits the same, such as 22, or numbers ending in a zero. You could ask many number questions linked to the topics being explored. The following are some examples.

• Find any number which has two of the same digit.

• Find the number that is the same as the number of wheels on your car.

• Find a number that matches the number of things you have in your collection.

• Find the number of your house/flat.

• Find the number which shows your age.

• Find the number which shows the number of people in your home.

• Find a number larger than 10.

• Find the number that matches today's date.

• Find the number that matches your birthday.

Number squares can also be used for board games, and children can practise counting along the rows, although in these cases the numbers need to be arranged as follows so that children can flow between successive lines when counting.

1	2	3	4	5	6	7	8	9	10
20	19	18	17	16	15	14	13	12	11
21	22	23	24	25	26	27	28	29	30
40	39	38	37	36	35	34	33	32	31
41	42	43	44	45	46	47	48	49	50
60	59	58	57	56	55	54	53	52	51
61	62	63	64	65	66	67	68	69	70
80	79	78	77	76	75	74	73	72	71
81	82	83	84	85	86	87	88	89	90
100	99	98	97	96	95	94	93	92	91

If children are offered number squares where the numbers are arranged in different ways, they will learn to not always expect the same presentation of resources; this means that they won't become over-reliant on any one resource but can learn to use a range of resources flexibly.

Critical question

» *What kinds of models and images are in your setting/classroom that can support children's visualisation and strategies for calculation?*

Comment

While it may be convenient to concentrate on a small number of pieces of equipment, children do need a wide range of models and images to support their calculation strategies. Some adults assume that young children do not need to be introduced to larger numbers, as they aren't expected to use them yet. However, children benefit from being introduced to large numbers early on, as they can then gradually become familiar with them, so that when they do need to calculate with large numbers, they are more likely to feel confident rather than anxious about the size of the numbers.

Specific adult-led activities for exploring calculation

The following are activities that an adult can plan and prepare for a small group of children to encourage them to look closely at calculation, building on the ideas in chapter 2, and get familiar with the processes of calculating through exploration and talk. Although these are adult-led activities, they don't have to be formally structured; rather than adhering rigidly to your initial plans, let the children's interest guide the activities.

• *Apple tree calculations.* Between 1 and 10 removable apples are displayed on a tree.

To encourage children to see the number bonds to 10, ask them questions such as:

If we add one more, how many would we have?

If we take one away, how many would we have?

If we have six apples, how many more would we need to make ten?

If we have eight apples and we take two away, how many would we have left?

- *Partition the number.* Have children make a book of the different ways to partition a given number, such as 8, and record what the patterns look like. They might also take pictures and add a number sentence or a recorded voice-over commentary.

- *Story of a number.* A number is chosen by either the teacher or the children, and children collect number sentences associated with the chosen number. For example, if 6 is the chosen number, then the sentences might include $3 + 3$, $8 - 2$, $12 \div 2$ and 3×2, which all have the answer 6. This gives children opportunities to explore the relationships between the arithmetic operations $+$, $-$, $\times$ and $\div$.

- *Problem solving with calculations.* In this activity children solve clues to the identity of a number. You can divide the class into small groups, and give each group three envelopes containing clues. For example, in one envelope there could be a card that says 'the number is twice 3', in another the card might say 'the number is 2 less than 8', and in the third the clue might be 'the number is an even number'. The children would check and compare the answers to each of the questions on the cards to ensure that they have the correct number. Each group could be given a different set of clues so that they are finding different numbers.

- *Combining dice.* Throw large dice and ask children to do calculations (depending upon ability) based on the numbers shown. With a pair of dice, you can ask for addition and subtraction calculations. If one dice is thrown, you could ask the children to double or halve the number.

- *Large targets.* Draw a large target on the ground or on a sheet of paper placed on the ground; the target should be large enough for children to stand on each of the sections.

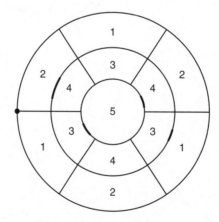

A target number is chosen, and children have to stand on the target to make up that number. For example, if 20 is the chosen number, five children could stand on the following sections: two on 5, two on 4, and one on 2 (so $2 \times 5 + 2 \times 4 + 1 \times 2 = 20$). The numbers on the target can be changed, as can the chosen total, so this activity can be used again and again without requiring extensive preparation. It is a good activity to do outdoors.

- *Repeated patterns.* Use a large-faced calculator or calculator on an interactive whiteboard to explore the patterns of numbers obtained through repeated addition or repeated subtraction. Either start with a small number and repeatedly add the same number on the calculator, for example $1 + 2 = 3$, $3 + 2 = 5$, $5 + 2 = 7$ and so on, or start with a large number and take away the same number each time, for example $60 - 6 = 54$, $54 - 6 = 48$, $48 - 6 = 42$ and so on. Ask children to predict what the next number will be and to explain how they have arrived at their answer.

- *Jumps of different sizes.* Here we model repeated addition by jumps on a number track. For example, if you use a number track big enough for children to stand on, a child could start on 1 and jump two spaces to land on 3, then jump another two spaces onto 5, and so on. An adult or another child can record the numbers on which the jumper lands either on paper or on a board for all to see, and then the pattern can be discussed. Jumps of different sizes can be investigated and the resulting number patterns explored. This activity, once introduced by an adult, can be left out for children to explore on their own as part of the continuous provision in the setting. The children may want to place toys on the landing numbers to show the pattern on the number track.

- *Hoop-la.* Children stand at a marked position and throw rings over skittles or plastic bottles. Each bottle has a number on it, and before each child throws, a card is drawn from a small pile which shows another number. If the child gets the ring over a bottle, they score the number that results from multiplying the number on the bottle by the number on the card. For example, if 3 is drawn on the cards and the child throws the ring over a bottle with 5 marked on it, the child scores 15 points. Strategies for working out the scores can be explored with the children. Observe whether anyone has worked out the answer differently.

Activities as part of continuous provision

In addition to specifically planned activities, there should be resources available in locations around the setting from which the children can choose, enabling them to explore calculating.

- *Skittles.* Children try to knock all the skittles down while being encouraged to calculate: How many skittles have been knocked down? How many more are there to knock down? How many have been knocked down after three attempts? The resources required include skittles, small balls, marked lanes, scoring sheets, paper and pens. Extensions could include marking each skittle with a different score so that children can add the scores for individual skittles they have knocked down and work on strategies for gaining the maximum number of points.

- *Large dominoes.* Children can match the dots on the dominoes or determine which end has the larger number of dots. They can identify similarities and differences between the dot patterns.

- *Safe darts*. Real darts have sharp points which can be dangerous, but there are safe darts that can be used with young children. The darts can be magnetic or have velcro on them so that they will stick to the dartboard. Children have to add together the numbers that the darts land on to keep score. Provide a whiteboard or blackboard and chalk for children to record their scores. Instead of using a traditional dart board that requires doubling and trebling the numbers scored, you could design other types of dartboards with different numbers on them.

- *Big snap*. Play snap with large cards, where some cards show number sentences and others show the corresponding answers. Children have to match together the number sentences and answers.

- *Fishing for numbers*. Set up a large 'pond' containing 'fish' with numbers on them. Children hook the fish by using a loop and hook, magnets, or velcro (depending on how the fish are designed). Give children a target number, and they need to hook any combination of fish to make that number. Each child's fishing results are recorded on a whiteboard or flipchart, showing addition of the numbers to make the target. A variation of this game could involve children fishing for a large number and then a smaller one to take away from it to leave a small target number.

- *The animals go two by two*. This game is linked to the story of Noah's Ark. Provide game boards with two each of various toy animals (or cards with animal pictures) placed on them in different squares. Children throw a dice to move their counter around a board and collect an animal when they land on the right square. The goal is to collect two of each animal. The winner is the child who collects all pairs on their board. A range of individual boards with different types of animals in pairs should be made available for the children to play with.

Play environments for children to explore calculating

Different kinds of play environments provide children with opportunities to explore specific aspects of mathematics as well as to use mathematical language appropriately and reinforce their skills. As a teacher, you need to be aware of how children might exploit these opportunities for incidental reinforcement of skills such as sorting shapes or for learning new ideas that arise naturally in the play context. Although initially you may set up an area for children to explore, it is important that they be able to add to and develop the environment as they play, changing the emphasis according to their needs and interests. The following ideas are meant to provide starting points for creating your own play environments. Play areas focusing on calculation alone could be quite boring and uninteresting, so the main goal here should be to create an environment that will stimulate the children's curiosity.

Pairs shop

Idea

In this shop environment, children identify pairs of items and group them to practise counting in twos.

Equipment

Find pairs of items to stock the shop, such as pairs of socks, shoes and gloves. Some of the items could be displayed on a washing line in the shop. For extra interest, the stocking of the shop could be undertaken by the children.

Outcomes

Children will talk about the meaning of 'a pair'. They will count in twos with different items. They can record the pairs of items that are sold in the shop.

Quad shop

Idea

This shop is stocked with items that have four, or a 'quad', of something, such as four sides. Examples might include chairs with four legs and toy cars with four wheels.

Equipment

Collect items with four of something. Again, the children can help to stock the shop.

Outcomes

Children will count the fours to check whether an item can be sold in the shop. They can record the items with an element of four that are sold in the shop.

Spells and potions

Idea

Make a wizards' or witches' cave where spells and potions are brewed. Provide recipes for spells and potions where amounts of ingredients must be added together or multiples of items are needed.

Equipment

Create a cave-like environment in one corner of the room. Provide several cauldrons or large pots in which the ingredients of recipes for spells and potions will be mixed. Make recipe cards for the spells and potions; these should offer opportunities for children to practise addition, subtraction, multiplication and division, and can be varied according to the interests and abilities of the children.

Example recipe: speed spell

Take one car with four wheels.

Add one share of nine counters shared between three children.

Take a pair of smelly socks.

Mix thoroughly.

This will make the person drink very quickly!

Children might need images to support their reading of the recipes.

Outcomes

Children will need to count items and identify or calculate the correct number needed for a recipe. A wizard or witch might sell a potion or spell to people who wish to gain special abilities. Children can also write their own recipes for potions and spells, recording the amounts of items with mathematical mark making.

Assessing children's skills

Can children:

- add one more to a given quantity;
- add two or more quantities together;
- subtract one from a given quantity;
- subtract one amount from another;
- share a given quantity equally;
- group a given amount into equal piles?

Test your subject knowledge

Try the following and think about how you are completing the calculations.

1.   83 + 46 =
2.   163 + 85 =
3.   732 + 24 + 143 =
4.   53 − 27 =
5.   163 − 97 =
6.   816 − 725 =
7.   seventeen multiplied by five
8.   90 × 3 =
9.   87 × 6 =
10.   84 ÷ 7 =
11.   112 ÷ 2 =
12.   876 ÷ 9 =
13.   17.37 + 8.57 =

Extend your subject knowledge

The grid on the next page shows the place value of each digit in a number given to three decimal places.

» Use the grid to help you work out the value of the specified digits in the following numbers.

(a) What is the value of the 9 in 6279?

(b) What is the value of the 1 in 2129?

(c) What is the value of the 2 in 2099?

(d) What is the value of the 7 in 2.47?

(e) What is the value of the 9 in 26.90?

(f) What is the value of the 4 in 10.914?

The grid illustrates the fact that the position or place identifies the value of the digit. Many people are taught to multiply decimal fractions by moving the decimal point. In reality, however, it is the digits that move their positions, while the decimal point remains fixed. For example, see how I've used the place value grid to multiply and divide the number 12.7 by multiples of 10.

Note that when multiplying by 100, we move every digit two places to the left; when dividing by 100, we move every digit two places to the right. In both cases, a '0' place-holder was inserted in the units place.

Now try some calculations for yourself.

» (a) $57 \times 10 =$

(b) $456 \times 10 =$

(c) $1.4 \times 10 =$

(d) $6.4 \times 100 =$

(e) $1700 \div 100 =$

(f) $64,300 \div 100 =$

(g) $1.2 \div 10 =$

(h) $3.200 \div 100 =$

Critical learning points from this chapter

» Calculating is a complex area for children to learn and is made up of a number of key components.

Millions	Hundred thousands	Ten thousands	Thousands	Hundreds	Tens	Units	.	Tenths	Hundredths	Thousandths	
					1	2	.	7			× 100 becomes
			1	2	7	0	.				

Millions	Hundred thousands	Ten thousands	Thousands	Hundreds	Tens	Units	.	Tenths	Hundredths	Thousandths	
					1	2	.	7			÷ 100 becomes
						0	.	1	2	7	

»   Children need to understand the relationship between the different operations of arithmetic.

»   Children need to understand why things work as well as how to complete calculations.

»   Children need to have opportunities to calculate using different items in different contexts in order to practise calculating accurately.

»   Children need guidance to help them develop their calculating strategies.

»   Children need to be given opportunities to record their calculations in their own way.

Critical reflection

Observe children when they are calculating and note the strategies that they use. What do you notice about their strategies? For example, are they using adding processes for both addition and subtraction? What kinds of strategies might you decide to model for these children? How might this information be used to plan the next steps for the children's learning?

Listen carefully to children's talk about calculating in play situations. Again, how might you use this information to assess their skills and plan the next steps in their learning?

Consider creating a play environment that has a clear mathematical focus to encourage children to calculate and record their reflections as part of the play.

Taking it further

Askew, M, Brown, M, Rhodes, V, Johnson, D, Wiliam, D (1997) *Effective Teachers of Numeracy*. London: King's College.

   This report highlights the skills needed to be an effective teacher of numeracy.

Gray, E and Tall, D (1994) Duality, Ambiguity and Flexibility: A "Proceptual" View of Simple Arithmetic. *The Journal for Research in Mathematics Education*, 26(2): 115–41.

   This is a key article about the establishment of the term 'precept', and is well worth reading.

Haylock, D and Cockburn, A (2008) *Understanding Mathematics for Young Children*. London: Sage.

   In particular, chapters 3, 4, 5 and 6 discuss calculating.

Skemp, R R (1976) Relational Understanding and Instrumental Understanding. *Mathematics Teaching*, 77: 20–6.

   This is one of the most cited articles in mathematics education; it stimulates everyone to think about how they learnt mathematics while at school.

References

Gray, E and Tall, D (1994) Duality, Ambiguity and Flexibility: A "Proceptual" View of Simple Arithmetic. *The Journal for Research in Mathematics Education*, 26(2): 115–41.

Ofsted (2011) *Good Practice in Primary Mathematics: Evidence from 20 Successful Schools*. Manchester: Ofsted, Crown Publications.

Skemp, R R (1976) Relational Understanding and Instrumental Understanding. *Mathematics Teaching*, 77: 20–6.

7 How can I say that?

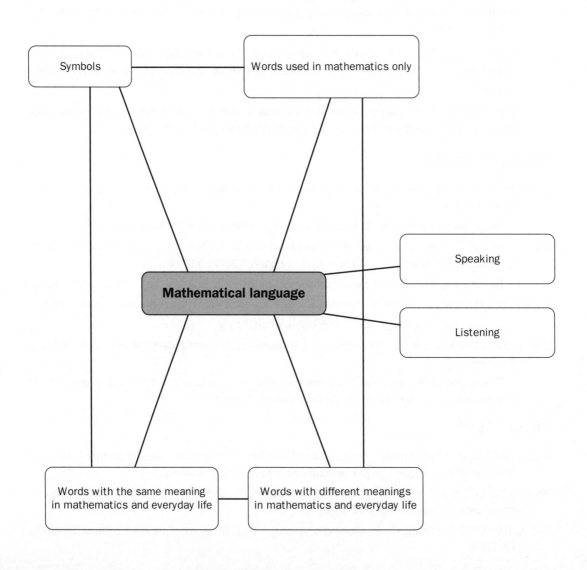

Introduction

> Mathematics education begins in language, it advances and stumbles because of language, and its outcomes are often assessed in language.
>
> (Durkin and Shire, 1991, page 3)

This chapter looks at children's understanding of mathematical language and some of the difficulties they might encounter. It also unpacks adults' understanding of children's prior experiences and discusses the impact this has on the development of children's ability to speak mathematically. Research over the past forty years has indicated that, in most settings, adults do the majority of the talking, which is dominated by asking questions through an 'initiation, response and feedback' (IRF) cycle (Flanders, 1970; Sinclair and Coulthard, 1975). Research in this area began with investigating adults' talk to children, along with the power and control exerted through such communication by the adults. The focus then shifted towards child-to-child interactions and how children talk with each other to establish shared understandings. Barnes and Todd (1977, 1995) considered the types of talk used by children when adults are not present and how these types affect the construction of meaning during group interactions.

It is important to remember that learning to speak mathematically involves using words that:

- have the same meaning in mathematics as in real life – for example, 'rule' and 'addition';

- have different meanings in real life and in mathematics – for example, in everyday life the word 'difference' means the physical discrepancies between items, but in mathematics 'difference' means the numerical deviation between numbers, eg, the difference between 7 and 3 is 4;

- are specific to mathematics and which may be completely new to children – for example, 'decimal'.

Young children's experiences of mathematical language

Schiro (1997) states that mathematical language includes reading, writing, speaking, listening, drawing and gesturing. He suggests that children

> encounter mathematical experiences; learn mathematics; enter the community of mathematical discourse; communicate their mathematical thoughts; personalize mathematics; express mathematical ideas; construct and articulate mathematical meanings for themselves and share them with others; remember mathematics; assess mathematical ideas; make connections; and relate mathematics and the world of the imagination and beauty.
>
> (Schiro, 1997, pages 73–4)

He also believes that when using stories for learning and teaching, the mathematics could be missed or misinterpreted if it is not made explicit by the adults. This is a key issue to keep in mind later in this chapter, when we discuss using children's books to teach mathematical language.

Children use contrast to discover meanings, and they also use their own experiences to make sense of language in different contexts. They bring these experiences with them to mathematical activities, which may lead to some misconceptions. The following are a few examples of situations that may arise.

The phrase 'take away' is used in calculation as another way of expressing subtraction, but children's everyday experience of 'take away' may have more to do with fast food, so they may associate these words with the local Chinese restaurant, fish-and-chip shop or McDonald's.

The word 'leaves' is used to express the result of a subtraction calculation, but initially children may confuse it with leaves on trees.

'More' is used in mathematics to show an increase in amount, but children's everyday experience may lead them to think this word means 'less'. This may seem strange from an adult's perspective; yet when we think about what often occurs in a child's life, we can begin to see why children might make this link: imagine that as a child I am having a treat like ice cream or chocolate; when asked if I would like *more* and answering yes, I usually receive a smaller amount than I was originally given, so now I have *less* than I had the first time.

'Difference' is a very tricky word for children to understand and use correctly, as in mathematics it is used specifically to mean a numerical difference between amounts. Children, however, tend to focus on visual differences, so if they are asked what the difference is between 3 and 7, some might say 'three is more curly', which for them is a perfectly logical statement to make, even though it doesn't employ difference in a mathematically accurate sense.

Two other words that have different meanings in everyday life and in mathematical contexts are 'odd' and 'table'. In everyday usage 'odd' means strange or different, but in mathematics it means a number which is not divisible by 2. In mathematics a 'table' is an organised display of data, not an object that you sit at to have tea.

Children need time, plenty of experiences involving the use of appropriate language, and reinforcement and modelling from the adults around them in order to develop their mathematical vocabulary.

English can be confusing

The English language can be confusing for children, especially around words that sound the same (homophones) but do not have related meanings. An example which affects counting is the confusion around 'two', 'too' and 'to'. The meaning of 'two' can be confused with the similarity of words and objects, so children may see a pair of shoes and say 'shoe shoe' rather than 'two shoes'.

Instructions can also be confusing

Children can also become confused by the language used in instructions for mathematical activities. For example, they may have trouble with instructions such as 'Draw a line between...', 'Ring' or 'Find two different ways to...'. This is most often a problem in written assessment tasks. Children need assistance in understanding these kinds of instructions, which, again, may have different meanings in mathematics than in other areas of the curriculum.

Symbols

A key difference between mathematics and other curricular areas is the use of symbols; as a consequence, mathematics moves towards abstraction more quickly than other subject areas. Boero et al, in a review of research on mathematics and language, stress the importance of natural language as *a mediator between mental processes, specific symbolic expressions, and logical organisations in mathematical activities* (Boero et al, 2002, page 243). Children use informal symbols early on without having to record them on paper; they use fingers to represent quantities from one to many; they can also invent symbols to represent quantity (see chapter 2 for more details). Mathematics in the classroom, though, emphasises a formal and abstract language.

Writing mathematics down using the conventional formal symbols presents potential difficulties for young learners. As part of learning to speak mathematically, children must first learn how to read the symbols and understand what they mean. Young children learn symbols for numerals and how these work in the base-ten place value system as part of early counting skills. Pimm (1991) writes that these symbols illustrate the structure of mathematics and assist learners in making manipulations routine; they also enable reflection about mathematics and facilitate a 'shorthand' way of recording mathematics. The symbols are not just abbreviations for specific words or phrases; they are ways of representing mathematical concepts which, in turn, are connected to other symbols and can be manipulated by adhering to specific rules. The meanings of symbols are also dependent on the situations in which they are used, and this makes navigating through the reading and understanding of symbols difficult for young children.

The research of Martin Hughes (1986) showed that it was the symbolisation of mathematics in formal mathematics recording that caused difficulties for young children. He also showed that children generally do not interpret the + sign as representing a 'symmetrical' relation between two sets. Children see this symbol more as a sign for action to be taken, in this case to make a number *more* by adding another number to it. Another example is the symbol =, usually read as 'equals', which means 'is the same as' or 'is equivalent to'. When children first meet the = symbol, they view it as an instruction to perform an action and so may read it as 'makes' or 'leaves'; only later, when an answer is found, will they see it as an equivalence. Resnick (1986) suggests that children with a high aptitude for mathematics are able to make sense of how symbols are used and the associated rules, and this makes them more successful in learning mathematics. Many commercially produced worksheets have a tendency to introduce formal symbols early. If children are introduced to symbols without understanding, misconceptions can arise and produce barriers to progress in mathematical learning. Children need to move from their own ways of recording (see the discussion on mark making in chapter 2) towards formal recording, through seeing the rationale of being able to communicate clearly with others using a standardised language that everyone will understand. As children become familiar with using mathematical symbols, they develop what Munn (1997) describes as mathematical 'literacy', which is essential for their continued mathematical development.

Critical question

»   *Look around the setting/classroom for numerals and symbols that are displayed for children. What are these numerals and symbols?*

Comment

You may think that young children only need to be exposed to a small range of numerals and symbols, as they are not yet expected to be using them in their mathematical learning. However, displaying a variety of numerals and mathematical symbols so that children become familiar with them is the equivalent of surrounding children with plenty of printed materials to support literacy development. We can support children's mathematical development by 'mathematising' their environment from early on.

Books and mathematics

Children's books can provide a springboard for children to discuss mathematical ideas and communicate mathematically using appropriate vocabulary. Through sharing books, children can explore counting, shape and space, and problem solving. The following are examples of books that could be read to children to stimulate discussion about mathematical ideas.

Book details	Key ideas	Examples of questions to ask children	Possible activities after reading
1, 2, 3 by Brian Wildsmith (2000)	This is a simple picture book about counting from 1 to 10.	Can you count the items on this page? Can you find the same number of objects in the classroom as on this page?	Children can make their own counting book, possibly linked to the current theme or topic in the setting; for illustrations you might take pictures or use the children's drawings.
One Hundred Hungry Ants by Elinor J. Pinczes (1999)	One hundred hungry ants head towards a picnic to get food. On the way they stop to change their line formation, showing different divisions of one hundred.	What would happen if there were a different number of ants (say 12, 24 or 30) going to the picnic? How could you show the different ways these ants could march? How could you use bricks or other items to model the line formations of the ants?	Create an insect corner with ants or other insects sorted into formations. You could also provide different kinds of containers and challenge children to find out how many insects would fill a specific container.
A Place for Zero: A Math Adventure by Angeline Sparagna Lopresti (2003)	Zero goes on a journey to discover his value.	Can you find the zero?	Draw maps of Zero's journey. Find zeros on a zero hunt. Make a grid to show place value from units through to thousands.

Book details	Key ideas	Examples of questions to ask children	Possible activities after reading
How Big is a Million? by Anna Milbourne (2007)	Pipkin the penguin is asking questions and wants to know how big a million is. This is his journey to explore numbers.	What is the biggest number that you know?	What does 20, 50 or 100 look like? Choose a number and make sets of different objects all with that same number. Find large numbers in books, newspapers, etc. to make a display.
Can You Count Ten Toes? Count to 10 in 10 Different Languages by Lezlie Evans (2004)	Ten different languages are introduced and written phonetically as well as in the language script.	Who can count in a language other than English? Can you teach us to count in your language?	Learn to count in different languages. Make a display about counting in different languages.
We All Went on Safari: A Counting Journey Through Tanzania by Laurie Krebs (2003)	A group of children set out on a journey and encounter different animals which they count.	Who can count these animals? How many more would be needed to make ten?	Find out about Tanzania and draw maps of the journey. Make friezes of different numbers of animals from the book.
The Greedy Triangle by Marilyn Burns (2008)	This story explores where triangles might be found in everyday life and begins to look at why.	Who can find the triangles in this picture? What other shapes can you see?	Design a world just for triangles. Children can write their own stories about different shapes.
The Great Pet Sale by Mick Inkpen (2006)	This story is about the animals in a pet shop being sold off at different prices.	How much for the dragon? If I had 50p, how much change would I get after buying this animal?	Set up a pet shop with soft toys as the pets and prices for each of them.
Actual Size by Steve Jenkins (2011)	This book illustrates the actual size of specific animals and other objects.	Is this bigger or smaller than...?	Measure the size of animals or other objects that interest the children.
Cluck O'Clock by Kes Gray (2010)	This book is about telling the time.	What time do you wake up? What time do we come to Nursery/school?	Make a frieze of the times when key things happen during the day.
A Fair Share by Stuart Murphy (1999)	This book is about sharing.	How could we share these sweets? How could we share these pieces of fruit?	Plan a party and share out the food for all the children.

Critical question

Schiro (1997) suggested criteria by which to evaluate books for potential use in developing children's mathematical skills; appropriate books are ones that:

» *are able to engage children in both mathematical and literary experiences;*

»   *allow children to respond to the story and the mathematics embedded in the story, as well as the quality of the presentation of both;*

»   *allow children to reflect on mathematical and literary meanings related to the book;*

»   *allow children to construct an understanding of the book's mathematics and story, as well as to view themselves as critics and problem-solvers.*

Look around your setting/school and review the books that are available. How could these be used to explore aspects of mathematics? How do they match Schiro's criteria?

Comment

The range and choice of books is likely to vary depending upon access to resources. If the selection is limited, you might consider making some books in collaboration with the children.

What do we know about the research on talk and mathematical learning?

Research in the USA shows that there is a significant relationship between the amount of mathematics-related talk by pre-school teachers and the growth of mathematics knowledge over the school years in the children they taught. Children do not learn simply by doing; they learn also through thinking and talking about what they are doing, and this is the key reason for using mathematical talk (Klibanoff et al, 2006). Children use such talk to begin to make connections between different aspects of mathematics; they try out their ideas and test out their understanding.

The research of Alexander (2004) explored teacher-led interactions with children and the different ways in which teachers could make use of dialogue in the classroom when interacting with children. From this emerged 'dialogic teaching', which he suggests is indicated by certain features of classroom interaction, such as the following:

-     questions are structured so as to provoke thoughtful answers;

-     answers provoke further questions and are seen as the building blocks of dialogue rather than its terminal point;

-     individual teacher–pupil and pupil–pupil exchanges are chained into coherent lines of enquiry rather than left stranded and disconnected.

(Alexander, 2004, page 32)

Other work in the UK has focused not on the individual children but, rather, on the talk that occurs in small groups of children working together. This has led to the identification of three different 'modes' of talk:

- disputational mode – characterised by disagreement and decision making at an individual level;

- cumulative mode – consists of positive but uncritical decision making;

- exploratory mode – seen to be the most effective for fostering critical thinking and cognitive development. In this mode of talk the children share all the information with all members of the group; children explore a range of solutions and test out hypotheses, and decision making is the result of critical argument and agreement.

(Mercer, 1996)

Adults working with children often feel that they need to intervene if discussions get heated, as disagreements are generally seen as negative; however, it is worth keeping in mind that exploring different perspectives is important for learning to progress.

Listening to children

Article 12 (Respect for the views of the child): When adults are making decisions that affect children, children have the right to say what they think should happen and have their opinions taken into account.

(UNICEF, 1989)

As well as engaging in conversations with children about the mathematics they are learning, it is important that adults working with children listen carefully to what children actually say. Through listening to children, it is possible to hear explicitly the connections they are making and plan appropriate learning experiences to assist progression in their learning. This also allows adults access to misconceptions that children may be developing and to plan to mediate those in the early stages of a child's mathematical development when they are easier to remove or change. Listening is a key skill to develop when working alongside children, especially in regard to the quieter ones who may not volunteer their ideas as readily as others.

Listening to children also means giving them space to explore their ideas in mathematical play and in problem-solving activities such as those discussed in chapter 5. Giving young children a voice is important for them to feel not just heard but that their opinions are valued; this helps adults to meet individual learning needs and to work with different styles of learning.

Critical question

» *How does your setting/school allow for young children to have their voices heard and valued?*

Comment

There are three issues to consider here:

Issue	Possible existing activities	Suggested alternative activities
Collecting children's views in fun ways that get their attention and do not just become part of the routine	Thumbs up to show everyone understands, or a similar checking-out activity before children go off to engage with other activities where their attention is on what they will do next. Passing a stone, wand or similar object around a circle to allow each child to have their say; the object can simply be passed on if the child does not wish to say anything.	Give children a set time to feed back on activities completed in a small group, using a sand timer to limit the time for each child to talk. Rate new activities available in the setting on a chart next to the activity, and then change those with low ratings to show children that their opinions matter.
Being open to what children say and valuing their views as part of a holistic picture of the children's experiences	Asking if children enjoyed activities, perhaps recording their emotional responses in photographs or jotted notes	Use journals focusing on activities both in the setting/school and at home, along with rating scales for children to complete in collaboration with their parents/carers.
Recognising that listening isn't just about hearing but also includes picking up on body language, especially from the youngest children or those not proficient in English	Additional space set aside for children to discuss ideas and issues either in small groups or individually	Closely observe the body language of children during activities, and afterwards engage them in discussion about what you have noticed.

Specific adult-led activities for exploring mathematical language

The following are activities that an adult can plan and prepare for a small group of children to encourage them to think carefully about the mathematical language that they employ. Although these are adult-led activities, they don't have to be formally structured; rather than adhering rigidly to your initial plans, let the children's interest guide the activities.

- Use simple games such as 'I spy' that children may already know, giving the games a mathematics-related theme so that children have to think about the initial sounds of shapes or numbers, for instance.

- Play 'I am thinking of a number', another language-based game where one person thinks of a number and the rest of the group ask questions to find out what that number is. The person who has chosen the number can only answer yes or no to each of the questions.

- In an alternative version of the previous game, a chosen child wears a hat with a number on it which they can't see but the rest of the group can. The child with the hat attempts to find out what the number is by asking the others in the group questions.

- Explore how shapes fit together to form pictures or larger shapes. This offers an opportunity to practise using the vocabulary associated with shape and space. You might use a tangram as the basis of this activity.

- Talk about a poster or picture. Show children a very detailed picture or poster and ask them to describe what they can see – for example, 'I can see three ducks', 'I can see a sail on a boat and the sail is shaped like a triangle'. This encourages children to look closely at items and describe them accurately so that others can get a good idea of what they are seeing.

- Use one of the books suggested earlier in the chapter or another suitable text as a starting point for discussions about the mathematical areas introduced in the book. Acting out the story – especially if it is about a journey, such as *We're Going on a Bear Hunt* (Rosen, 1997) – gives children practice in using positional language.

- Look for numbers in the newspaper and discuss what they mean. Choose a number appropriate for the age group, and ask children questions like 'Does it include zeros?' or 'How is it written?'

- Have children explore items in feely bags and then describe them to the rest of the group. This encourages children to use appropriate mathematical language accurately. The feely bag can be filled with 2D and 3D shapes, number shapes, or other interesting objects to be described.

- Create shape stories – give every child a shape; then go around the group, asking each child to add a line to the story that includes something about their shape. For example, the first child might say, 'Ben met a triangle which has three sides', and then the next child might add, 'He also met a square which has four corners'. All contributions to the story must include properties of the shape.

- An alternative version of the previous activity is to fill a shopping basket: each child adds an item to the basket which must have a mathematical aspect, eg, four bananas, a pentagon.

- Create a slideshow of mathematics-related pictures and ask children to provide an oral commentary to accompany the slideshow.

- Model the use of symbols to write number sentences, and discuss the similarities and differences of related sentences, such as $2 + 3 = 5$ and $3 + 2 = 5$, or $5 - 3 = 2$ and $5 - 2 = 3$. These could be accompanied by pictorial representations of the number sentences, enabling the children to see the connections between pictures, symbols and language. The idea here is to introduce the symbols and for the children to explore their understanding in an oral context initially before undertaking any formal recording.

- *Odds and evens*. This game is played in pairs, with one child taking 'odds' and the other 'evens'. They both place their hands behind their backs, clenching their fists, and after the count of 1, 2, 3 they bring their hands to the front and open one or both fists to show a number of fingers. If the combination of the number of fingers is an even number, the 'evens' child gains a point, and if the combined number of fingers showing is odd, then the 'odds' child gains the point. The first child to reach ten points is the winner.

- *Positional snap*. For this activity you need a set of cards with positions illustrated on the cards – about four of each position. Shuffle and play as a usual snap game. 'Snap' is called when the cards match, and the winner must be able to say what the positional word is, eg, 'down'.

- *Positional bingo*. For this activity you need a set of baseboards which either have words to cover with pictures or have pictures to cover with words. Each baseboard must be different. The caller shuffles a set of cards and draws one card at a time until someone has covered their entire baseboard.

- *The order problem*. Children work out where to place toys in a queue by reading clues and placing the toys in the correct order. Sample clues might look like:

The doll is last in the order.

The teddy is next to the soldier.

The ball is first in the order.

The teddy is behind the ball.

The soldier is in the middle of the order.

You can extend this activity by making longer queues with more clues, or the children could form an order in a line and write clues for others to solve.

Activities as part of continuous provision

In addition to specifically planned activities, there should be resources available in locations around the setting from which the children can choose, enabling them to explore mathematical language.

- Any of the play environments below can be used to encourage children to talk about what they are doing. A recording device could be provided so that children can record themselves and others with whom they are playing.

- Provide a space with pens and a whiteboard for children to act as 'teacher'. The 'students' could be toys or other children. This environment would allow the children to rehearse their mathematical language.

- Provide recordings of nursery rhymes and stories which include mathematical elements, along with headphones or a quieter area where children can listen to the recordings.

- Give children access to pre-recorded instructions for building with blocks. Listening to such instructions helps children learn positional language.

- *Shadow drawing*. Place two easels back to back. A child draws something on one easel and then describes the item without directly naming it; another child draws on the other easel according to the description given by the first child. Then they can compare drawings.

- *Weather records*. Have children record the weather once or twice a day. Information about different aspects of the weather can be collected each day. (See also the weather centre play environment below.)

Play environments for children to explore mathematical language

Different kinds of play environments provide children with opportunities to explore specific aspects of mathematics as well as to use mathematical language appropriately and reinforce their skills. As a teacher, you need to be aware of how children might exploit these opportunities for incidental reinforcement of ideas. Although initially you may set up an area for children to explore, it is important that they be able to add to and develop the environment as they play, changing the emphasis according to their needs and interests. The following ideas are meant to provide starting points for creating your own play environments.

Pet shop

Idea

Set up a pet shop with various kinds of (toy) animals, appropriate-sized homes for the animals, food and equipment, together with the prices of everything.

Equipment

Soft toys; cages, carrying containers, baskets, bedding; bags of pet food, water bottles; money, a till; pen and paper for stock taking and checking on animals in the shop. You could also make a display of the care requirements for specific pets, ie, what they need in terms of homes, food, toys and general care.

Outcomes

Children will choose specific pets and match appropriate homes and equipment to the pets. They will use money to purchase pets, homes and food. They might check to see how many pets will safely fit into a carrying case. There will be discussions between the children serving in the shop and the children playing customers. Children acting as shop assistants will check the stock in the shop. Children can sort pets according to their size, needs and cost. This environment encourages the use of mathematical language.

Plumbers

Idea

Set up a plumbing business where plumbers talk to customers about their requirements. Children can be encouraged to think about measuring pipework to move water from one point to another. This would be a suitable activity for outdoors, especially in warmer weather.

Equipment

Tape measures, clipboards, paper, pens, lengths of pipework, tools and overalls. If doing this activity outdoors, children should be given suitable protective clothing so they can avoid becoming soaking wet.

Outcomes

Children can be observed discussing customer requirements and collaborating on problem solving. Here you are likely to see if children understand how to connect pipework so that water will flow between two given points. Children may record the measurements made and discuss with other plumbers how they will solve the problem of getting water from one location to another.

Games centre

Idea

Set up a games centre where children can come to play selected games that explore different aspects of mathematics.

Equipment

Games such as dominoes, cards, snakes and ladders, matching games, table-top skittles, bagatelle and any others available. You could also provide score boards for children to record their results.

Outcomes

You may observe collaboration between children, as children who know how to play the games teach others the rules. Discussion will focus on rules, turn taking, reading dice or other scores, calculating running scores, and what is needed to win a particular game. Here you are likely to see if children understand how the rules apply to turn taking. Children may record their scores. They may also wish to bring their own games into this environment and explain to others how these work. Young children can also explore their ideas about fairness and likelihood in connection with the games played.

Weather centre

Idea

Set up a weather centre where children can record the weather, plan broadcasts of the weather forecast, draw maps and take weather measurements such as rainfall and wind direction.

Equipment

Paper, pens, easels or flipcharts, rain gauge, maps, perhaps a mock-up of a television studio for giving weather forecasts, and possibly a camera/camcorder for either pretend or actual recording of the programme.

Outcomes

Observe the extent to which children collaborate in planning their weather forecasts and how they will present them. Discussion will focus on observations of the weather outside and measurements such as temperature, rainfall and wind direction. Children may record the information collected. They will begin to link their experiences with weather to the need for suitable clothing and activities.

Assessing children's skills

Can children:

- talk about the shapes of everyday objects using appropriate language;
- talk about how they have carried out their calculations;
- use positional language to describe the relationship between themselves and objects or between two objects, or to tell stories about journeys;
- use appropriate mathematical language to describe logically the rules of games;
- use appropriate mathematical language when working with measures;
- use appropriate mathematical language when talking about their approaches to problem solving;
- understand the symbols used to record mathematics;
- make connections between symbols, pictures, practical situations and mathematical language?

Test your subject knowledge

Find out the mathematical and non-mathematical meanings of the following words:

prime, median, mean, mode, product, combine, dividend, height, difference, example, operation

Extend your subject knowledge

» Use a mathematics dictionary to check out mathematical terms and their correct definitions before you introduce them to children.

» Display posters of mathematical terms in the setting that children and adults can use for reference.

Critical learning points from this chapter

» Language is key to children exploring their mathematical ideas.

» Using the correct mathematical terms from the beginning is very important in helping children to develop their understanding.

» Listening to children is an important way of gaining information about their understanding of mathematics.

» Listening to children is important for acknowledging their needs and wishes.

» Adult-to-child and child-to-child communications are equally important to the learning process.

» Symbols can be difficult for children to understand and use in their move from the concrete to the abstract.

Critical reflection

Observe who does most of the talking during mathematical activities – adults or children? How could you increase the space for children's voices?

Reflect on how much adults listen to children when working on mathematical activities.

What resources/equipment/environments are there in your setting/school already that will allow children to explore opportunities to use mathematical language? Look particularly at stories as a resource for mathematics learning.

Annotate children's recording with extracts of what the children have said to inform discussions with children and their parents/carers.

Plan an environment that encourages children to make use of their mathematical language.

Taking it further

Housartt, J and Mason, J (eds) (2009) *Listening Counts: Listening to Young Learners of Mathematics.* London: Trentham Books.

> This book looks specifically at listening to counting and children's talk about mathematics in the home environment and in Early Years and school settings.

References

Alexander, R (2004) *Towards Dialogic Teaching: Rethinking Classroom Talk*. Cambridge: Dialogos.

Barnes, D and Todd, F (1977) *Communication and Learning in Small Groups*. London: Routledge and Kegan Paul.

Barnes, D and Todd, F (1995) *Communication and Learning Revisited: Making Meaning Through Talk*. Portsmouth, New Hampshire: Boynton/Cook Publishers, Heinemann.

Boero, P, Dreyfus, T, Gravemeijer, K, Gray, E, Hershkowitz, R, Schwarz, B, Sierpinska, A and Tall, D (2002) Abstraction: Theories About the Emergence of Knowledge Structures, in Cockburn, A D and Nardi, E (eds) *Proceedings of the 26th Annual Conference of the International Group for the Psychology of Mathematics Education*, Volume 1, pp 113–38. Norwich: University of East Anglia School of Education and Professional Development.

Burns, M (2008) *The Greedy Triangle*. New York: Scholastic.

Durkin, K and Shire, B (1991) *Language in Mathematical Education: Research and Practice*. Milton Keynes: Open University Press.

Evans, L (2004) *Can You Count Ten Toes? Count to 10 in 10 Different Languages*. Boston, Massachusetts: Houghton Mifflin Harcourt.

Flanders, N (1970) *Analyzing Teacher Behavior*. Reading, Massachusetts: Addison-Wesley.

Gray, K (2010) *Cluck O'Clock*. London: Hodder Children's Books.

Hughes, M (1986) *Children and Number*. Oxford: Blackwell Publishers.

Inkpen, M (2006) *The Great Pet Sale*. London: Hodder Children's Books.

Jenkins, S (2011) *Actual Size*. London: Frances Lincoln Children's Books.

Klibanoff, R S, Levine, S C, Huttenlocher, J, Vasilyeva, M and Hedges, L V (2006) Preschool Children's Mathematical Knowledge: The Effect of Teacher "Math Talk." *Developmental Psychology*, 42: 59–69.

Krebs, L (2003) *We All Went on Safari: A Counting Journey Through Tanzania*. Oxford: Barefoot Books.

Lopresti, A S (2003) *A Place for Zero: A Math Adventure.* Watertown, Massachusetts: Charlesbridge Publishing.

Mercer, N (1996). The Quality of Talk in Children's Collaborative Activity in the Classroom. *Learning and Instruction*, 6: 359–77.

Milbourne, A (2007) *How Big is a Million?* London: Usbourne Publishing.

Munn P (1997) Children's Beliefs About Counting, in Thompson, I (ed) *Teaching and Learning Early Number*, pp 9–19. Buckingham: Open University Press.

Murphy, S (1999) *A Fair Share*. New York: Harper Collins.

Pimm, D (1991) Communicating Mathematically, in Durkin, K and Shire, B (eds) *Language in Mathematical Education: Research and Practice*, pp 17–23. Philadelphia: Open University Press.

Pinczes, E J (1999) *One Hundred Hungry Ants*. Boston, Massachusetts: Houghton Mifflin.

Resnick, L B (1986) The Development of Mathematical Thinking, in Perlmuter, M (ed) *Perspectives on Intellectual Development: The Minnesota Symposia on Child Psychology*, Volume 19, pp 159–94. Hillsdale, New Jersey: Erlbaum.

Rosen, M (1997) *We're Going on a Bear Hunt*. London: Walker Books.

Schiro, M (1997) *Integrating Children's Literature and Mathematics in the Classroom: Children as Meaning Makers, Problem Solvers, and Literary Critics*. New York: Teacher College.

Sinclair, J and Coulthard, M (1975) *Towards an Analysis of Discourse*. Oxford: Oxford University Press.

UNICEF (1989) The UN Convention on the Rights of the Child, available at www.unicef.org.uk.

Wildsmith, B (2000) *1, 2, 3*. Oxford: Oxford University Press.

8 How do I record this?

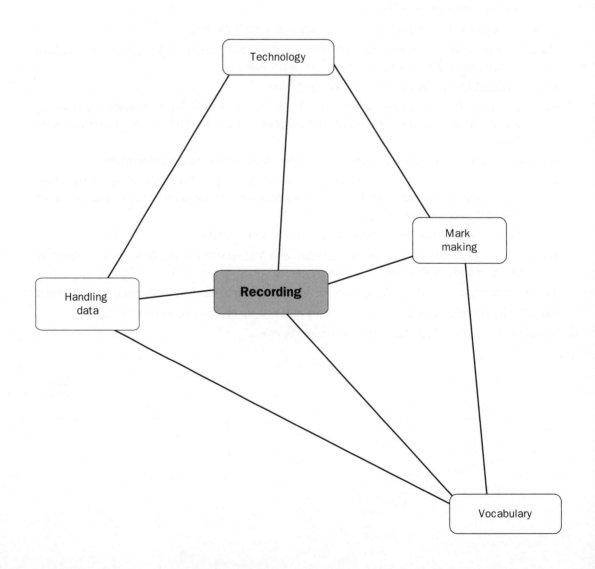

Introduction

This chapter looks at children's recording of mathematics and builds on the mark making explored in chapter 2; it will also address the area of handling data, as data is often recorded in a number of ways in the Early Years. Mathematics can be viewed as a language which children need to learn. In chapter 7 we discussed the oral language of mathematics and the need for children to be introduced to and get familiar with using correct mathematical vocabulary. Recording mathematics is a big step in the move from a concrete understanding of activities towards an abstract understanding of mathematical ideas such as 'numeral', which can embody or represent a range of understandings about number. Pimm (1987) suggests that writing or recording mathematics *externalises thinking even more than speech by demanding a more accurate expression of ideas* (Pimm, 1987, page 115).

The race to record can be seen as a 'political' one, as mathematical recording provides apparent evidence of children's achievements; however, this can occur at the expense of children's complete understanding, and may represent a move towards rote learning. It can be easier for parents and others to understand what children are learning in mathematics if they can see a greater connection with what is recorded. Children's mark making may not be easy for adults to interpret without a full understanding of the learning process. The brevity of formal recording is seen as a mark of success in the learning of mathematics as it is universally recognised and understood.

Numerals

Numerals are important symbols for children to recognise and use in mathematics. In chapter 2 the focus was on counting and the move from counting to calculating. In this chapter, we focus on the recording of mathematical ideas; numerals are one way of recording ideas about quantity, for example. This doesn't mean that children have to start learning numerals by recording the numerals themselves. It can be a gradual process, beginning with matching numerals prepared commercially or written by adults to groupings of that number of items; this allows children to link numerals to counting and sorting.

When children do begin to record numerals, it is worth considering, as an initial guide, the research related to handwriting within the area of literacy. Activities that support early handwriting skills can also support numeral formation. The following is a list of suggested activities:

- copying shapes;
- colouring, writing, painting, or using jelly and cornflour to make shapes and numerals;
- writing big numerals – eg, tracing them outside on the ground or inside in the air;
- making large-scale numerals outdoors using a variety of materials;
- collecting different representations of numerals (eg, in different fonts) – for example, ask children to find all the '3's they can from pictures in magazines, or to take pictures of numerals on doors or anywhere else they occur;
- matching numerals to sets to assist recognition of numerals.

Just as with learning to write, children need to be observed while they are forming numerals – check that they start and finish in the correct places and that the orientation of the numeral is correct. Children can reverse numerals in the same way as they reverse letters. Research by Medwell and Wray (2008) suggests that handwriting that has become automated frees the writer to concentrate on composition. Although numeral formation has not been researched in the same way, it is possible that once numeral formation has become automated, children will be able to concentrate more easily on the processes of mathematical thinking, as they no longer need to focus their efforts on forming numerals correctly when recording their ideas. The formation of numerals requires children to have a mental image of the symbol and an understanding of left–right orientation. The easier numerals to write are 1, 3, 4, 5 and 7, while the circular movements required for 6 and 9 make these harder to master; the numeral 2, with its combination of straight and curved lines, is generally even harder to form, and the numeral 8 is most difficult because of the cross-over movement at the centre. As a result, children often try to write an eight by forming two circles and connecting them with various degrees of success. Lucangeli et al (2012) carried out a longitudinal study in Italy, focusing on children from three and a half to five and a half years old, to examine how children arrive at correct representations of numerals. They identified five paths to correct numeral writing, which they described as: 1) linear, 2) forward and backward, 3) no symbols, 4) symbols, and 5) an early number developmental path. The work of Lucangeli et al took as a starting point the ideas of Hughes (1986) and Carruthers and Worthington (2005) discussed in chapter 2; they showed that young children have different pathways to representing numerals and that adults working with young children need to acknowledge these differences and take them into account when planning the next steps in children's learning. Adults need to help children make the transition from using their own representations of quantities to using the formal numerals, and learning to write these correctly is an integral part of that process.

Critical question

» *Consider the research described above and what it means for your practice. What do you currently do to support children's transition from their own mark making to the use of formal numerals? What activities do you use to help children learn how to form numerals correctly? Do you begin with the numerals you know children find easiest, or do you concentrate on learning the pattern of numerals alongside counting so that children are always writing the numerals in order?*

Comment

In light of the research about which numerals children find easiest to write, you might consider working with children to master those numerals first, rather than trying to teach the order of numerals at the same time as writing numerals. If you don't currently link the ideas of fluency from handwriting research with writing numerals, you might consider using good practices for teaching handwriting to support children's formation of numerals.

Other kinds of recording

Children can record what they have been doing in a wide variety of ways, which can include the sorts of mark making discussed in chapter 2 as well as formal recording with numerals and other symbols. In the early years, adults can be more flexible in the range of recording options that they offer children to engage with or explore in more depth. Giving children a choice as to how they might record their thoughts about mathematical problems allows children space to have their voice heard. The latter could be achieved quite literally by making a digital sound recording of a child or children talking about a mathematical activity; the recording could be accompanied by children's drawings or photographs of what they are talking about.

Some alternative recording methods are:

- talking and making a sound recording of the descriptions/ideas;
- drawing;
- painting;
- taking photographs;
- physical modelling, which can include 'people mathematics' such as children physically forming sets;
- making models;
- creating a visual record of what has been completed, eg, sorting items into groups, showing the difference between numbers on a number line or track;
- creating a visual display on a velcro wall or similar environment.

The following table shows how children might use these types of recording methods in specific activities.

Type of recording	Examples of activities where the recording method would be helpful to record children's ideas
Audio recording	Measuring in a sand and water tray and recording the count of cups to fill a container. Providing a running commentary of a journey through a trail.
Drawing	Performing a subtraction calculation, for example by drawing the original set and showing how many items have been taken away. Showing a specific shape (eg, a triangle) or a set of objects (eg, five toys, my favourite 10 things).
Painting	Describing the journey a programmable toy has taken. Displaying a number of items collected.
Taking photographs	Identifying the group of children who like apples. Describing the shape of a window. Displaying a particular number of items.
Physical modelling	Children forming groups according to a category identified. Children making the shapes of numbers with their bodies. Physical graphing of preferences.
Models	Creating a model just using cubes and cuboids. Constructing a maze for programmable toys to navigate.

Type of recording	Examples of activities where the recording method would be helpful to record children's ideas
Creating a visual record	Sorting a set of objects into categories. Presenting a calculation using equipment such as cubes, counters or other counting resources.
Creating a visual display	Collecting everything that a child can find associated with the number three. Displaying all the things that a child can find associated with length.
Mark making	Children using their own recording methods, such as drawings, tallies, letters and numerals.
Using numerals and symbols	Recording the results of a calculation. Showing the difference between numbers; this might include displaying pegs on a number line or track.

Specific adult-led activities to encourage and develop children's recording skills

These are designed to be short activities which can be undertaken indoors or outdoors to encourage children to record their ideas.

- *Matching numerals to sets of objects*. Prepare large numerals on cards. Children count sets of objects and then match the number of objects in each set to the corresponding numeral card.

- *Adults scribing words for children*. To show children how recording might be done for any given task, adults can scribe what children say to annotate models, pictures, etc. For example, if children have been asked to create models using cuboids, the adult can ask each child to describe their model and perhaps what they did to construct the model; the adult then writes down or types the child's description.

- *Audio recording*. An example would be to ask children to make repeating patterns outdoors. Each child then talks about their pattern and is recorded while doing so. The digital audio files can accompany photographs of the patterns to make a slideshow that could be shared with a larger group.

- *Taking pictures and adding text*. This is similar to the previous activity, and could be linked to a shape walk where children find shapes along the walk and describe what they are seeing. Children can take pictures of the walk and the shapes they have found, and then add text to explain their reasons for taking each photograph and the connections between the different pictures. The text could be created by the children themselves, or adults can type or write down what children say. The pictures and text could be collated in Word files or Powerpoint presentations. These can then be used as the basis of discussions about shapes to reinforce ideas and correct any misconceptions.

- *Making large numbers outside*. Children model large numbers outdoors, either individually or in small groups. and their models stand as a record of the activity. Images of the models could be captured using a camcorder or camera to provide a more long-term record of the children's activity.

Activities as part of continuous provision

In addition to specifically planned activities, there should be resources available in locations around the setting from which the children can choose, enabling them to explore aspects of recording mathematical ideas. Paper, pens, crayons and other writing and drawing implements should always be available to children. It is also helpful to give children access to a camera, tablets and audio recorders that they can use to record their thoughts by audio or visual means.

Play environments for children to explore recording mathematical ideas

Different kinds of play environments provide children with opportunities to explore specific aspects of mathematics as well as to use mathematical language appropriately and reinforce their skills. In the environments suggested below, the focus is on recording. Although initially you may set up an area for children to explore, it is important that they be able to add to and develop the environment as they play, changing the emphasis according to their needs and interests. The following ideas are meant to provide starting points for creating your own play environments.

Junk shop

Idea

Create a shop that is full of interesting things for children to explore and sort in the role of either shopkeeper or customer. As an added stimulus, a story could be read to the children to start them thinking about how to organise items in the shop, such as *The Ship-Shape Shop* by Frank Rodgers (1994).

Equipment

Collections of interesting objects that could be sorted or organised in different ways; a wide variety of containers, such as baskets, boxes and bags, into which the sorted items can be packed; maybe also a till and money.

Outcomes

In the role of shopkeeper, children can decide how to organise the items in the shop; they will also sort, store and keep track of the items. As customers, the children can select items from the shop to explore and create patterns with. Both roles afford opportunities to record activities such as sales, stock taking and pattern making.

Fast food cafe

Idea

Create a fast food cafe where children can purchase burgers, chips, nuggets, salads, shakes, soft drinks and fruit bags. Roles that can be played in this environment include the people taking orders from customers, cooks and food preparers, and people sweeping and tidying the seating areas.

Equipment

A few small tables and chairs, waste bin; pretend food for the cafe to cook and sell; tills and money, charts to record sales of particular items; small bags for chips, boxes for burgers; menus of items that can be requested from the cafe along with their prices, list of special orders or combinations.

Outcomes

As order takers, the children can decide how to record the orders and the costs of the meals requested. As customers, the children can select items from the menu or the list of specials and pay the appropriate amount of money. The cooks and food preparers can refer to the orders to prepare, cook and serve the food requested. Sales can be recorded in different ways by all those participating in the play environment.

Estate agents

Idea

Create a scenario where children have to record a range of attributes of properties for sale. Provide a clear rationale for the need to record information in this situation.

Equipment

Ideally, you would set up a number of dolls' houses; these could either be made especially for this play environment, or you could use commercially produced dolls' houses. The estate agents would need tape measures, pens and clipboards to measure and record details about each of the properties, including the size of each house, the number of bedrooms, whether there is a garage, other key features of the house, and whether it is for sale or to let. You could prepare a sheet like the example below on which children can record the information they have collected, or you could allow the children to devise their own recording method. To make the estate agents' office more authentic, you could furnish it with desks, chairs, computers, telephones, possibly a photocopier, a diary for house-viewing appointments, and maybe even some means of transport to take people to view the houses.

House for sale or rent		Address and telephone number
Picture of house		
Location	**Number of rooms**	**Notes**
Ground floor		
First floor		
Outside		
Other information		

Outcomes

The estate agents will take pictures of the houses and display them. They can decide on the prices of houses for sale or the rent to be paid. They will arrange and record appointments, viewings and sales or rental agreements. They will record information about the properties, including any measurements. They will copy details for people interested in buying, selling or renting. The customers will ask questions about the houses for sale or rent, make appointments to view some of the houses, and be shown around the properties.

Assessing children's skills in recording

Can children:

- talk about their mathematical activities;

- draw or paint to show what they have been doing;

- take a photograph to record their activities;

- show their mathematical thinking through modelling;

- represent their recording with mark making;

- use numerals appropriately to record mathematical ideas;

- use mathematical symbols to record their ideas?

Critical question?

» *Consider the mathematical recording you do in your everyday life as an adult, either at home or at work. Does this look like the mathematical recording you were taught at school? When does it look the same as formal recording and when is the recording more informal? What makes the difference in the format of the recording?*

Comment

In informal situations, adults tend to use shortcuts developed over time, including simplified ways of recording mathematical ideas and calculations for themselves. When communicating with others or in more formal situations, we choose the universally understood, formal symbols and recording methods to help facilitate the communication process.

Handling data

Handling data is often taken to mean representing information in formats such as graphs, pie charts and pictograms. It encompasses a far broader range of activities, though. Part of it is about sorting, classifying and organising information in various ways, which could include tables and graphs. Most people stop at this representation stage, missing out the most crucial part of handling data, which is the interpretation, explanation and discussion of the information gathered.

There are five key steps in handling data, sometimes collectively referred to as the data-handling cycle.

1. *Pose or specify the problem to be solved* – this can be a simple question, such as 'What is the most popular fruit?'

2. *Plan* – decide what data is to be collected.

3. *Collect the data* – determine how the data is going to be collected and then collect it.

4. *Process and represent* – take the raw data collected in step 3 and present it in a suitable format.

5. *Interpret and discuss* – return to the original question and decide how can this be answered using the data collected.

Leavy (2008) conducted a review of the research on young children's statistical understanding, drawing heavily on the work of Jones et al (2000), which identified three levels of statistical thinking: level 1, idiosyncratic; level 2, transitional; and level 3, quantitative. They concluded that children who demonstrate an idiosyncratic level of understanding draw on their own experiences and make interpretations that are not necessarily supported by the data. Children at the transitional level will look at the data more closely but not always see the relationships within the data. This research offers a way to describe how children understand statistics at a given stage of development, and can be helpful for assessing their understanding and planning the next steps in their learning.

Critical question

» *Many people using statistics end the data-handling process at step 4, 'Process and represent'. Why do you think this happens?*

Comment

At school, considerable time is usually spent on learning the mechanical skills of constructing graphs and charts, especially in the days before graphical calculators and computers became widespread; therefore, limited or no time was available to focus on interpretation of the data. Partially as a consequence of this, many people see the presentation of the data as the end product, and they may think that the data will speak for itself if it is represented in the right way. The problem is that graphs, charts and tables used to summarise data often don't include sufficient information to allow the viewer to make a reasonable judgement about what is being shown, or to interpret and discuss what the data says about the research question posed. For example, this pie chart shows two things occurring at proportions of 50 per cent each.

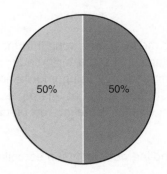

» The chart does not contain sufficient information to enable us to judge the results revealed by the data. For a start, it would be useful to know the size of the population from which the data was collected. If this was a population of 10, one might wonder why the information was presented in this way, as 10 is a very small population size. If the population was 1000, the fact that it is evenly split can be descibed much more effectively in words; the pictorial representation does not provide any further useful information and is not needed.

» The following example is a better use of the pie chart.

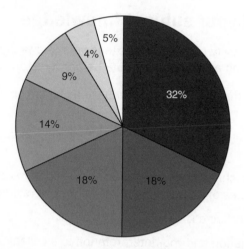

» This pie chart contains more detail, but it still needs an indication of the population so that the viewer can get a holistic picture of the situation. It should also have a key to tell the viewer what each section of the pie represents. To complete the data-handling cycle, we need to add a few lines interpreting the data being represented: What does the data tell the reader? What does it mean?

» The same is true of other forms of representation, such as the bar chart below.

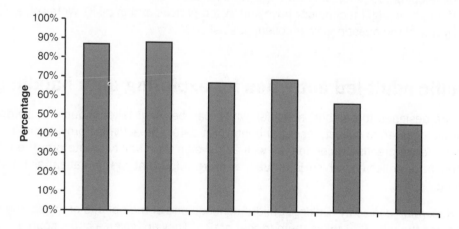

» Here, again, there is some crucial information missing. The vertical scale or y-axis is marked in percentage terms, but there is no indication of what the horizontal or x-axis *represents and what data is actually being collected. Furthermore, percentages may not be an appropriate measure to show on the vertical scale. For example, if the data collected was the amount of time children spent at specific activities in a nursery, with each of the bars representing a different amount of time, then the percentages (heights of the bars) should add up to 100%; but in this case the total is much more than 100%, so it is impossible to interpret and draw meaningful conclusions from this graph.*

Test and extend your subject knowledge

Complete the following activity to check and extend your knowledge of handling data. Make sure you re-read the section about handling data before you start work on this task.

1. Every five minutes throughout the day, choose a child to observe and record what they are doing.

2. Organise and prepare an appropriate way to represent the data from your observations.

3. Make sure that the chosen representation format contains sufficient information, eg, keys to the categories of data presented, to help viewers interpret the data.

4. Interpret the data collected.

5. Present the information and your interpretation to a colleague or small group of colleagues.

6. Answer any questions they have about the methods of data collection, recording, presentation and interpretation.

7. Ask your colleagues for feedback about the clarity of the information presented.

8. Reflect on the learning experience as a whole and plan any next steps required in developing your subject knowledge in this area. Did you use technology to help you? If not, how might technology have supported phases of this task? Were you surprised by any of the questions your colleagues asked?

Specific adult-led activities for exploring data handling

These are designed to be short activities which can be undertaken indoors or outdoors to encourage children to collect, record and interpret data. The activities provide children with opportunities to practise recording, as well as develop their ability to interpret the information they have collected, which is actually a more important mathematical skill than the recording.

- *Recording choice by walking.* Children choose one of the options provided and walk along the path that takes them to that option. They are given a cube, counter or card with their name on it, and they place this object at the end of their route to indicate their choice. For example, if the options are various toys, children follow a path to their favourite toy and leave their card, cube or counter there.

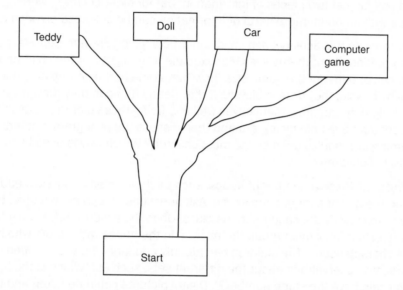

Once everyone has made a choice, count the cards, cubes or counters for each choice. The data is then interpreted: Which toy is the group's favourite? Which toy is the least popular? To begin with, you could provide only two choices; then increase the number of choices as the children become familiar with the process.

- *Data cards.* Each child is given a card on which they put information about themselves. You can vary the kinds of information requested. The following is an example.

Self portrait

Age

Name

Brothers
Sisters
Cats
Dogs

Favourite
colour

Favourite food

Then sort and organise the information collected and decide how it could be presented. Finally, discuss and interpret the results. For the youngest children you could ask for just two pieces of information, but for older children, working in small groups with an adult, more sorts of information can be collected on each card.

- *Pictograms.* In this activity each child constructs a pictogram to represent a piece of information about themselves. For example, you might ask the children to draw, on pieces of paper of the same size, how they come to the setting or school. If they come by bicycle, they draw a bicycle; if they get a lift in car, they draw a car; and if they walk, they can draw themselves walking. Using these pictures, the children and you construct a simple pictogram and then discuss the pictogram created: Which way of coming to school is used by the most children? Which way is used by the smallest number of children?

- *Sorting sets.* Place a number of hoops, such as those used in physical education, around the hall or a large open space. Ask questions – such as 'Who has brown hair?' – to classify the children in the class. Once the children have considered each question, they must group themselves in the hoops with others who have the same characteristics. The children can identify and label the sets created. They can also record observations about the different sets, such as: 'Which is the biggest?', 'Which sets have the same number?'. Digital pictures could be taken and placed in slideshow presentations with titles and appropriate statements, or they could be used to make a display or book about the class. This demonstrates a visual method of recording activities as well as a practical approach to handling data.

- *Sorting tray graphs.* Prepare a labelled sorting tray like the one shown.

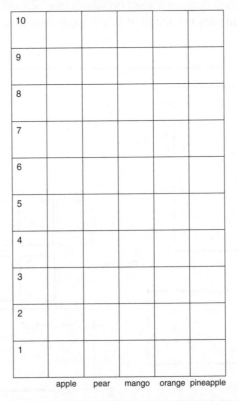

Children create a graph in the sorting tray by placing an object such as a counter in one of the spaces corresponding to their choice. For example, for the tray shown above, the data collected would be the favourite fruit of each child, so each child places a counter in a space above their favourite fruit. This activity acts as a method of both data collection and data representation. When completed, the resulting graph can be interpreted and discussed.

Play environments for children to explore data handling

Different kinds of play environments provide children with opportunities to explore specific aspects of mathematics as well as to use mathematical language appropriately and reinforce their skills. In the environments suggested below, the focus is on handling data. Although initially you may set up an area for children to explore, it is important that they be able to add to and develop the environment as they play, changing the emphasis according to their needs and interests. The following ideas are meant to provide starting points for creating your own play environments. In each there is a clear rationale for collecting and organising data. The activities also involve recording ideas and offer opportunities for reinforcing other skills such as counting and sorting.

Weather station

Idea

Create a weather station for taking measurements each day of the weather outside the setting/school.

Equipment

A rain gauge to measure rainfall; a weather vane to show wind direction; a thermometer to measure the temperature; a chart against which to judge the amount of cloud in the sky; charts on which to record the weather conditions outside; symbols that could be put on the charts to indicate the type of weather.

Outcomes

Children will observe and record different elements of the weather. They need to organise and display the data collected each day. They can also discuss and interpret the data collected.

Health clinic

Idea

Set up a clinic where data about patients is collected, sorted and organised. This could be linked to a project about growth and development, which could be explored across the curriculum.

Equipment

Scales for weighing babies and children, tape measures (care may be needed if some children are sensitive about their weight or height); paper and pencils for recording the measurements of patients; coats and stethoscopes for the doctors; aprons or uniforms for the nurses; charts for recording and comparing the measurements taken from different patients. You may also want to include prescription pads for medicines.

Outcomes

This activity could involve measuring length/height, weight, head circumference, body temperature and blood pressure. There will be opportunities for comparing measurements, mathematical mark making, and collecting, organising and interpreting data.

School or classroom

Idea

Create a school situation where children can take the roles of teachers or pupils. This could be connected with a trip to an old school room or a video/web conference with a school in another country, giving opportunities for cross-curricular work.

Equipment

Tables, chairs; paper, pens, whiteboard; registers, mark sheets, books; possibly stickers for rewards and star or sticker charts for individuals or classes.

Outcome

Children will collect data about attendance at school, staying for dinner or not, completion of homework, and marks or sticker rewards given for good behaviour or good work.

Theatre

Idea

Set up a theatre with seating for the audience and a stage area for performances; this could be a puppet theatre.

Equipment

Puppets; a stage, or blocks that could be used to form a stable raised area; numbered seats for the audience; a seating plan for the ticket office.

Outcomes

For each performance, tickets are sold or given away to children and crossed off the seating plan to ensure that tickets are only issued for the number of seats available. One-to-one matching of tickets to seats is undertaken by the child in the ticket office. There are opportunities to collect data from the audience about which performances they liked most and why.

Assessing children's skills in handling data

Can children:

- sort the data collected;
- organise the data collected;
- provide a description of the data collected;
- recognise a representation of the data collected;
- represent the data;
- interpret the data collected;
- discuss what a particular representation of the data tells them?

Test and extend your subject knowledge

1. To check your understanding of mathematics knowledge in the area of data handling, first write down what you think the following terms mean, and then check your definitions against a mathematical dictionary or the glossary section of this book.

    Bar graph

    Histogram

    Line graph

    Statistics

    Pie chart

    Percentage

    Range

2. Find a newspaper or news website and look at how statistics are used to convey information and how that can sometimes be misleading. Did you find any instances of mathematically incorrect usage of statistics, such as where percentages are discussed that add up to more than 100 per cent?

Critical learning points from this chapter

»   Recording can assist children in exploring their mathematical ideas.

»   Children can use a variety of forms to record their ideas.

»   Recording can assist children with visualising different models and images associated with mathematical ideas.

» Children can sort and organise data as part of recording information.

» The key aspect of handling data is the interpretation and discussion that comes after the representation of the data.

Critical reflection

Audit the opportunities available to children in regard to the variety of recording methods for their mathematical ideas.

What resources/equipment/environments are there in your setting/school that will allow children to explore opportunities to record their mathematical ideas?

Reflect on the kinds of recording that take place in your setting/school. What is the balance of adult recording and child recording?

Review the opportunities children have for collecting, organising and sorting data.

Annotate children's recordings from mathematical activities with extracts of what children have said to inform discussions with children and their parents/carers.

Plan an environment that encourages children to record their mathematical ideas.

Taking it further

Haylock, D and Cockburn, A (2008) *Understanding Mathematics for Young Children*. London: Sage.

    In particular, chapter 9 focuses on handling data.

Montague-Smith, A and Price, A (2012) *Mathematics in the Early Years Education* (third edition). London: David Fulton.

    In particular, chapter 7 is about handling data.

Worthington, M and Carruthers, E (2006) *Children's Mathematics: Making Marks, Making Meaning* (second edition). London: Paul Chapman.

    This book details the work on mathematical mark making undertaken by these two researchers and gives a wide range of examples of the mark making children use and the variety of contexts in which this occurs.

References

Jones, G A, Thorton, C A, Langrall, C W, Mooney, E S, Perry, B and Putt, I J (2000) A Framework for Characterizing Children's Statistical Thinking. *Mathematical Thinking and Learning*, 2: 269–307.

Leavy, A (2008) An Examination of the Role of Statistical Investigation in Supporting the Development of Young Children's Statistical Reasoning, in Saracho, O N and Spodek, B (eds) *Contemporary Perspectives on Mathematics in Early Childhood Education*, pp 215–32. Charlotte, North Carolina: Information Age Publishing.

Lucangeli, D, Tressoldi, P and Re, A M (2012) Path to Numbers Writing: A Longitudinal Study with Children from 3.5 to 5.5 Years Old. *Journal of Educational and Developmental Psychology*, 2(2): 20–31.

Medwell, J and Wray, D (2008) Handwriting – A Forgotten Language Skill? *Language and Education*, 22(1): 34–47.

Pimm, D (1987) *Speaking Mathematically: Communication in Mathematics Classrooms*. London: Routledge.

Rodgers, F (1994) *The Ship-Shape Shop*. London: Picture Puffin.

9 What does this do?

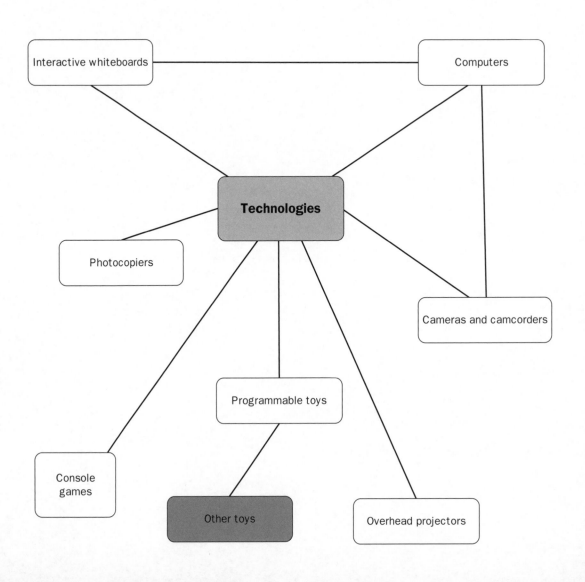

Introduction

This chapter looks at young children's use of different kinds of technologies – not just computers, which are often the first thing that adults think of when considering technology. In this chapter we will see how technologies can encourage an explorative approach and support discussions about mathematics.

Much of the discussion around children and information and communication technology (ICT) has focused on 'digital illiteracies', and the activities emphasised have mostly been storytelling and work in the arts with film-making. Roberts-Holmes (2013) finds that children do not have the same issues with technology as adults have and are happy to explore what various devices can do without worrying about making mistakes; they are able to work with the devices more intuitively. Prensky's (2001) term 'digital natives' supports this view that young children are often fluent in a 'digital language' that many adults don't speak. In many ways, this makes ICT a perfect vehicle for learning in mathematics, where often anxieties are created about getting the right answer. Parette et al (2010) argues that in the Early Years we are in danger of 'missing the boat' with the use of technology in developing learning and teaching. They are concerned that young learners will find it hard to keep up with rapid changes in technology if they not introduced to the technology at an early stage of their education while building on their experiences in everyday life: *Such experiences provide powerful models for technology use while also shaping the changing profile of our technology-based culture* (Parette et al, 2010, page 336).

This chapter will explore the benefits of technology and also highlight the need for a clear rationale for its use. Rather than employing technology simply because it is there, we need to think carefully about the match between task and purpose so that the most appropriate learning journeys are undertaken. No specific software or hardware is recommended in this chapter, as technology quickly becomes outdated and it is difficult to keep up with the rapid changes to hardware, software and apps. Therefore, the discussion in this chapter is about general principles. There are many websites listed in the 'Taking it further' section, which can provide starting points for additional ideas, software and apps that you might use in your activities with children. This chapter does not include any discussion of television, DVD or film technologies; although these may be used to enhance learning, the majority fall outside the area of mathematics learning and teaching.

Types of technological devices

Computers

Although computers are by no means the only technology around, they are worth discussing in the context of Early Years education, especially with the move away from static terminals to handheld devices such as tablets, which are much easier and more flexible for children to use. For both types of computers, software programmes or apps are available that focus on specific aspects of mathematics.

When deciding upon the kinds of software programmes that might be used with children, it is important to understand what the software is offering.

To begin with, software programmes and apps can be divided into two broad categories, each with advantages and disadvantages.

Type of software	Description/ examples	Advantages	Possible disadvantages
Content-free software	Packages which can be used with any curriculum area, such as Microsoft Word and Excel.	The context can be set by the teacher or the learners, so the packages are very flexible; also, skills learnt in using one package can be transferred to other programmes of similar type. These packages can be most useful in play environments for young children, as they allow the children to make choices about how to use them.	These types of software require more preparation from the teacher in order to make clear the links to specific areas of the curriculum. Teachers need to be able to see the connections themselves first. The packages need to be set up to emphasise the mathematical elements. In play situations, it may not always be obvious to the children what choices to make about how they will use the technology.
Content-specific software	Programmes with a mathematical theme, possibly focusing on key skills to match current expected curricular outcomes	These are often 'plug and go' packages which require little or no setting up and are therefore easy to make available to children. They often include instant feedback.	These packages can oversimplify the mathematics so that it either becomes just 'drill and practice' or gets obscured. In some of these packages it can be difficult or impossible to give an incorrect answer.

There are other ways of categorising the software that computers and tablets can run, such as the classification scheme shown in the following table. Adults need to think carefully about the purpose of each specific type of software before using it extensively in the classroom, as the different types will give very different kinds of experiences for the children using them.

Type of software	Description/ examples	Advantages	Possible disadvantages
Tutor	This kind of software is commonly referred to as a 'drill and practice' programme. The child has to choose or input the answer to each question and gets instant feedback. The feedback can take different forms, from a green tick or red cross to smiley faces and animations.	These kinds of programmes typically have a very clear structure, and both children and adults can find them easily accessible. They give quick feedback on the answers. They usually require little or no setting up and are ready to use immediately after installation. They give children opportunities to practise skills and apply knowledge already learnt.	With multiple-choice questions there are sometimes only a few options, so children can end up guessing or getting bored. The lack of variety means that such programmes can be a one-use activity, as children lose interest quickly. These programmes can be confusing when used for teaching, as they may use terminology or methods different from those introduced in the classroom.

Type of software	Description/ examples	Advantages	Possible disadvantages
Simulator	These programmes come in a variety of formats, from simple spreadsheets to adventure games.	The contexts of simulator programmes are often game-like environments, which can generate a high level of interest in children. They usually have a number of different levels and can be used again and again over a considerable period of time.	Sometimes the mathematics can be oversimplified or submerged in the context of the game. Children can get frustrated if the questions or tasks are too challenging and they are not able to proceed to the next level after many tries.
Tool	Software in this category is usually, though not exclusively, content-free. This includes writing, drawing, graphing and communication packages. It also includes web browsers.	The context can be set by the learner or teacher, so these are flexible packages.	These types of software require more preparation from the teacher in order to make clear the links to specific areas of the curriculum. Teachers need to be able to see the connections themselves first and plan carefully how the software will be used for learning.

There are software packages and apps available that will cover most aspects of the early years mathematics curriculum, but you will probably find that they tend to emphasise numerical skills, and give only limited attention to problem solving, unless it is in the form of 'word problems'. One major concern raised in a report by the Open University was that *many games were of low educational value* (Flewitt, 2012, page 7).

Software can be evaluated by looking at the positive attributes of the programme/app. The following table can be used to help you begin to evaluate critically the programmes/apps that are currently being used in your setting or which might be used in the future.

Positive attribute of software	Yes	No
Instructions for operating clear and simple, appropriate for the age group		
Instructions are provided on screen, either iconic or aurally or both		
A skill-building component is included		
The mathematics is explicit in the activities		
Promotes problem solving over rote learning		
The relationship between answer options and questions is not predictable		
Ideas and concepts are modelled in different ways for the learner, ie, there is not just one representation offered		

Positive attribute of software	Yes	No
Clues are available as an optional extra for the learner		
Allows learner to make mistakes		
Self-correction can lead the learner to the answer		
Offers appropriate feedback, including why any response might be incorrect		
Offers a motivating reward		
Offers the opportunity to restart the activity		
Offers a pause facility so that a learner can return to a programme later if they need or want to stop at any point		
Offers the opportunity to save at the point where any activity is completed to enable a return visit		
Offers a variety of levels of difficulty so that the programme can be used more than once		
The visual appearance is attractive		
The environments created relate to the children's world		
Any key sequence required is clearly explained, as are the functions		
Hand–eye coordination skills required are appropriate for the age group and the device		
There is a help function if needed		
The activity can be completed individually and independently		
The activity can be completed with one child and one adult		
The activity can be completed with a small group of learners		
The activity can be completed with a larger group of learners		

In summary, with appropriate software children can:

- individually practise skills such as counting;
- individually play games such as Sudoku or finding the way out of a maze;
- collaborate to play a mathematical game;
- collaborate to record outcomes of problem solving, eg, using Word;
- compete in teams to play a game;
- discuss presentations made by the teacher with Powerpoint and projection facilities.

Cameras and camcorders

As digital cameras and camcorders become more and more widespread, photography and video recording has become easier and easier for everyone. Nowadays children can usually access these kinds of devices easily. It can be very helpful for them to take their own pictures for:

- sequencing;

- following directions or routes, either filming or taking pictures where there are changes of direction;

- identifying shapes and numbers in the environment;

- recording the steps taken in problem solving;

- recording patterns created indoors or outdoors;

- recording the process of creating a pattern;

- displaying number sequences.

Listening devices

Most households have a device or devices for listening to music and spoken-word recordings, so children are usually very familiar with the use of this type of technology. With audio play-back devices, children can;

- listen to rhymes involving numbers, shapes, sequencing and order;

- listen to songs involving number, shapes, sequencing and order;

- listen to stories involving mathematics, which can be done at the same time as following the story in a book.

Interactive whiteboards

Many classrooms have interactive whiteboards, and many of these boards are just used for projecting from a computer – but they are much more versatile than that. There are two different types of interactive whiteboards.

- One type of interactive whiteboard is just an electronic version of a dry whiteboard which enables learners in a virtual classroom to view what is written or drawn on the board. This is sometimes called an electronic whiteboard, and is often found in conferencing and data-sharing facilities.

- Another type of interactive whiteboard is a large physical display panel that can function as a whiteboard (though with a different kind of pen), a projector screen, an electronic copy-board, or a computer projector screen on which the computer image can be controlled by touching or writing on the surface of the panel instead of using a mouse or keyboard.

Most educational institutions have the second kind of interactive whiteboard, often linked directly to a computer. The following table lists some of the advantages and disadvantages of interactive whiteboards.

Advantages	Disadvantages
Allow for greater child involvement in lessons or adult-led sessions. Allow children to work collaboratively on a task.	Front projection can mean that when someone is adding material to the board, others can't see what is going on. Can be placed too high for young learners to reach the board.

Advantages	Disadvantages
Interactive elements provide greater motivation and hold children's attention better. Allows more movement for kinaesthetic learners. Allows for highlighting to emphasise vocabulary or key elements of learning for all to see. Good for drag-and-drop activities. Can be used to play games where elements, such as numbers or shapes, have to be identified against the clock. Mistakes can easily be erased so that learners can try again.	Free-standing boards need realigning every time they are moved. Can be difficult to follow if a number of people are adding to the board simultaneously. Some products require different kinds of pens to be used, and this can be difficult for young children to remember. Motivating factors diminish with use. Depending upon lighting, the visibility of images on the board can be impaired. Can be costly to buy and maintain.

Somekh et al (2007) reviewed the implementation of interactive whiteboards in primary schools and, although finding many positives, they included this concern in their recommendations:

> serious consideration also needs to be given to developing strategies other than whole-class-teaching for using interactive whiteboards to support pupils of lower ability. Whole-class-teaching, especially when conducted at the increased pace made possible with an interactive whiteboard, does not address the specific needs of pupils who are not able to grasp the relationships between symbols and words or concepts without more individual help.
>
> (Somekh et al, 2007, page 10)

Although this research focused on the primary age range, the increase in larger-group teaching sessions also characterises many Early Years settings, along with changes in staff–pupil ratios and pressures on teachers and children to demonstrate progress in learning. It is therefore important that teachers consider the issue of the pace of learning using technologies, as it is too easy to assume that with the aid of technology, teaching pace can increase.

Photocopiers

Although photocopiers are not new technology, they are very useful in enabling children to explore questions about scale through enlarging and reducing the size of images. Encourage children to investigate what happens when they magnify or shrink certain shapes and to solve shape- and scale-related problems using the photocopier.

Overhead projectors

These can be very useful for:

*   enlarging images, numbers and shapes;
*   revealing shapes gradually for children to make predictions about the final shape;
*   showing number patterns with counters or blocks;
*   illustrating partitioning of numbers;

- illustrating sharing and grouping;
- demonstrating puzzles such as tangrams (where the area covered remains the same but the shape/picture changes).

Electronic readers

It is possible to download children's books to these devices, including many of the books with mathematical content mentioned in chapter 7. A wide range of free materials for children can be downloaded, from pictures to lengthy stories. Some electronic readers display in black and white only, but devices with colour screens are becoming increasingly common. There are also many apps available for reading ebooks and other electronic materials on computers, tablets and smartphones.

By using electronic readers, children can:

- find numbers;
- find shapes;
- discuss sizes and differences;
- count;
- read mathematical stories.

Programmable or remote-controlled robots and toys

Children and adults don't always consider the mathematical possibilities of using such toys, but they can be a good source of practical illustrations of mathematical knowledge. These devices can be used for:

- illustrating directions;
- showing turns;
- demonstrating the following of instructions;
- sequencing;
- problem solving, eg, finding the shortest route between two points.

Calculators

The use of calculators in educating children has been a hot topic of debates for many years, and there continue to be concerns about children's over-reliance on these devices to perform calculations. It is inevitable, however, that children will come into contact with calculators, either as individual items or integrated into other technology. There is no expectation that children be formally taught in the Early Years about how to use calculators, but these devices are one more piece of technology that children can explore further. Research has shown that availability of a calculator does not have a negative impact on children's ability to calculate. The critical issue is that children need to learn to use calculators effectively and be able to tell whether the answer they get on the screen is appropriate.

In the USA it is accepted that calculators should be part of the mathematics curriculum at all levels, and this message has come through their curriculum organisations, such as the National Council of Teachers of Mathematics (NCTM), which said that *appropriate instruction that includes calculators can extend students' understanding of mathematics and will allow all students access to rich problem-solving experiences* (National Council of Teachers of Mathematics, 1998). Later the NCTM further strengthened their statement to *technology is essential in teaching and learning mathematics; it influences the mathematics that is taught and enhances students' learning* (National Council of Teachers of Mathematics, 2000, page 24). In the UK, the Calculator Aware Number (CAN) project developed a suggested rubric for ways of working with calculators.

- Classroom activities should be practical and investigational, emphasising the development and use of language, and ranging across the whole curriculum.

- Encouragement should be given to exploring and investigating 'how numbers work'.

- The importance of mental calculation should be emphasised.

- Children should be encouraged to share their methods with others.

- Children should always have a calculator available.

- The choice as to whether to use a calculator should be the child's not the teacher's.

Moreover, Shuard et al make the following suggestions.

> Traditional written methods of calculation should not be taught.
>
> Children should use a calculator for those calculations which they could not do mentally.
>
> (1991, page 7)

The guiding principle behind the CAN project was that *[c]hildren should be allowed to use calculators in the same way as adults use them: at their own choice, whenever they wish to do so.* The project conducted extensive classroom-based investigations into children using calculators, and many of the ideas resulting from this research can be seen in subsequent developments in curricula, influencing not just the use of calculators but also the ways in which mathematics is learnt and taught in general.

Children can use calculators for:

- finding numbers;

- investigating number patterns;

- exploring what happens when particular keys are pressed.

Critical question

» *What are the difficulties with allowing children to use calculators in the Early Years?*

Comment

You may think that calculators encourage children to rely on technology for calculating, rather than learn to use mental calculation methods or formal written algorithms. However, there is no research evidence to support the view of over-reliance on calculators. To perform calculations accurately with calculators, the person inputting the numbers still needs to know how to enter the data correctly, and they must be able to tell whether the answer obtained is appropriate or not. One difficulty with allowing children to use calculators in the Early Years is that the adults might be unsure about how to guide the children and answer questions the children may ask about using this form of technology.

Other technological toys and devices

These might include phones, handheld game consoles, scanners, tills for shop environments, microwaves and cookers for kitchen environments. These can all be explored where appropriate for:

* identifying numbers;

* playing mathematical games;

* discussion of measures, including time;

* discussion of problem-solving strategies;

* sequencing.

Specific adult-led activities to encourage and develop children's mathematical skills through the use of technology

These are designed to be short activities which can be undertaken indoors or outdoors to encourage children to use technology to facilitate their learning of mathematics.

* Demonstrate the key features of a specific software programme or piece of technology that children might use in the setting. For example, adults could demonstrate a drag-and-drop game using an interactive whiteboard, and then children could explore the game later as part of the continuous provision.

* Shapes, groups of items or sequences of numbers can be drawn or printed on overhead transparencies and then uncovered gradually while they are being displayed on the wall by an overhead projector. Children can hypothesise about the shape, number of items or pattern of numbers that will be revealed when the whole transparency is uncovered.

* Use a photocopier to make a number of different-sized teddies while the children watch and collect the images. These can then be used for a discussion about sizes and how they could be compared and ordered.

- Discuss with the children the pictures they have taken with digital cameras. For example, ask about the shapes that are present in their pictures, the number of people in the picture or any numbers that can be seen in the image.

- Children demonstrate the use of a programmable or remote-controlled car or a favourite game, and the adults prepare questions that illustrate the mathematical skills the child is developing, helping them make connections between playing with technology and mathematical learning.

- Use an appropriate programme to construct a graph of children's likes and dislikes, for example in a fruit-tasting activity (first check for any allergies). If the data is entered as the children make their choices, they can see how the information changes with each new entry.

Activities as part of continuous provision

In addition to specifically planned activities, there should be resources available in locations around the setting from which the children can choose, enabling them to explore aspects of mathematics using technology.

- Set up a listening corner with audio recordings of mathematical stories, rhymes and poems, along with copies of the books. A variety of listening devices can be made available as well as electronic readers.

- Establish a calculating corner with calculators, tills, and tablets with electronic or writing calculators (these are apps for tablets such that if you write the calculation on the screen, the app will complete the calculation for you, changing your writing into print) for children to explore. Problems or challenges could be left for the children to solve – for example: 'Can you find the number 5 on each of the devices?', 'Can you fill the screen with the same number repeated?'

- Place cameras in a specific area with a daily challenge – for example: 'Take a picture of a set of four things.' A sticker prize could be given to the children who complete the task each day, and you could make a display of the collection of pictures associated with the task.

- Construct a maze through which remote-controlled toys could be steered, providing children with an opportunity to think about direction, distance and turns.

- Provide walkie-talkies that children can use to call each other between indoors and outdoors; this can help with number recognition.

Play environments for children to explore technology and mathematics

Different kinds of play environments provide children with opportunities to explore specific aspects of mathematics as well as to use mathematical language appropriately and reinforce their skills. As a teacher, you need to be aware of how children might exploit these opportunities for incidental reinforcement of skills such as counting or for learning new ideas that arise naturally in the play context. Although initially you may set up an area for children to explore, it is important that they be able to add to and develop the environment as they play, changing the emphasis according to their needs and interests. The following ideas are meant to provide starting points for creating your own play environments.

Computer office

Idea

Create a working office environment where children can explore how computer technology works.

Equipment

Computers, printers, whiteboards, tablets, digital cameras, phones, reading devices and calculators, as many as possible.

Outcomes

Children will explore numbers, shapes and patterns created on the different devices. There might be discussions among the children and between children and adults about the possible change in output from calculators if buttons are pressed in a different order. Children may use keyboards to record numbers, and they may use programmes to design and explore patterns. Children can form patterns, numbers and shapes on the whiteboard.

Wallpaper manufacturer

Idea

Create an office for a company that designs and manufactures wallpaper. The wallpaper could be for dolls' houses so that the quantities are not too large. Designs can be created by making repeated patterns of drawings or digital pictures scaled to the required size.

Equipment

Computers, tablets, digital cameras, photocopiers, printers, scissors and glue.

Outcomes

Children will discuss repeating patterns and how to cover different areas with such patterns. They will enlarge or reduce the size of images and copy them to make patterns.

Remote-controlled toy shop or hire shop

Idea

Set up a shop or stall where equipment can be hired that specialises in electronic and remote-controlled toys.

Equipment

Collect as many remote-controlled toys as possible, plus batteries to ensure that they all work. You might supplement this with other electronic devices for playing games. Provide uniforms or name badges for the shopkeeper and sales assistants, also paper, pens and clipboard for taking inventories, and possibly a till and money. Children could also play the role of guides to demonstrate and explain to customers how the toys work.

Outcomes

Children can create mazes or courses for toys to negotiate; the discussion will focus on directions and turning. This can be a good activity for assessing children's knowledge and skills through observing them at play and listening carefully to their conversations.

Children's kitchen

Idea

Set up a kitchen environment where children can either play with pretend electronic equipment or use real equipment to create sweets, biscuits or meals under adult supervision.

Equipment

For the pretend environment, collect as many pieces as possible of toy kitchen appliances that make noises, have timers, or include moving parts. For the real kitchen environment you could have equipment such as microwaves and cookers. You could also include a phone for children to talk on while they are cooking.

Outcomes

Children will press numbers and buttons to work the equipment and will talk about how long food needs to cook. They might answer the phone and take orders for the kitchen. They will measure out ingredients and count out plates.

FOCUS ON RESEARCH

Aubrey and Dahl (2008) reviewed the use of ICT in the Early Years and Key Stage 1. They found that while there was a wide range of technologies, hardware and software available specifically for this age group, there were differences in children's access. Increasingly, children encounter a wide range of technologies before attending a setting/school. The research found that adults' attitudes to these technologies were generally positive, that they actively promoted children's use of this medium for learning, and that this, in turn, had an impact on children's development.

Young children are confident with new technologies and are very willing to explore new gadgets that they have not encountered before.

(Aubrey and Dahl, 2008, page 4)

However, not all practitioners feel confident about using the technologies, with more feeling confident in maintained than in non-maintained settings; as a consequence, the report suggests that there is a training need. According to the research of Parette et al (2010), this is an issue in the USA also, as many of the training courses there in early childhood education did not include any compulsory elements related to ICT.

Critical question

»   *The research outlined above collected data from a range of groups – practitioners, children and parents. Read the following statement about parental views from the report, and consider what this might mean to you as a practitioner.*

Interestingly, the parents' survey revealed that they felt media education should be included in the school curriculum from when children were very young. They reported that they would welcome further work on new technologies in school, believing that their children needed to be prepared for the demands of the new technology age.

(Aubrey and Dahl, 2008, page 27)

»   *What is your response to this statement – do you think that technologies should be an integral part of the early years curriculum? What are the potential barriers to implementation?*

Comment

You may agree with the statement about integrating technologies into the Early Years curriculum but be concerned about the availability of hardware. Many settings have concerns about the cost of technology, and this can be a major barrier to the use of ICT in the Early Years. You may also have evaluated your own confidence and competence with technologies and feel concerned about how to work with children who may appear to know more than you do. You could treat this as a learning opportunity, if you ask children to show you what the equipment can do – though you might want to ask them to go slowly, as people often quicken the pace when they are dealing with things they find familiar. Do you and your colleagues review the use of technology in your setting? Are there staff members with more confidence and skill in this area who would be able to demonstrate to others?

Assessing children's skills

Here the point is not to assess children's ability to work with or understand particular technologies. Rather, we want to assess whether children can use technology to facilitate their learning of mathematics and to demonstrate their knowledge of mathematics in a different context.

Can children:

- talk about the shapes of everyday objects using pictures they have taken as source material for the discussion;

- use appropriate language to explain and justify their ideas when working with technology;

- recognise numbers on devices that they use, such as photocopiers and phones;

- identify patterns on whiteboards, computers or tablets;

- sequence pictures or patterns using photographs they have taken;

- make a film or take pictures to illustrate instructions;

- accurately talk about directions such as left, right, up and down when playing with programmable or remote-controlled toys?

Extend your subject knowledge

1. Audit your own subject knowledge in this area

Use the following rating scale:

1 = confident and competent

2 = reasonably confident and reasonably competent

3 = limited confidence and limited experience (could be a target for development)

Aspect for review	1	2	3
Computers			
Interactive whiteboards			
Tablets			
Electronic readers			
Listening devices			
Calculators			
Remote-controlled toys			
Digital cameras			
Digital camcorders			
Photocopiers			
Overhead projectors			
Other electronic toys and games			

2. Audit the technologies available in the setting

Use the following rating scale:

1 = a wide range available for staff and children
2 = reasonable amount available but could be increased
3 = limited availability for staff and children (could be targeted for development)

Aspect for review	1	2	3
Computers			
Interactive whiteboards			
Tablets			
Electronic readers			
Listening devices			
Calculators			
Remote-controlled toys			
Digital cameras			
Digital camcorders			
Photocopiers			
Overhead projectors			
Other electronic toys and games			

3. Evaluate the software/apps already in use in the setting

» Using the rubric from earlier in the chapter, take one software package, programme or app used in your setting and critically review how good it is. You might also invite a small group of children to join in with this activity and incorporate their views into the overall evaluation. Discuss your findings with colleagues: Do they agree? Where do any differences lie? What are the sources of differences of opinion?

4. Construct an action plan for your own development and for the setting

Focus for development	Priority: short, medium or long term	What actions are needed to achieve the development focus?	Support/ resources needed to achieve the development focus	Target date by which this development focus will be achieved	Who is responsible for implementing this development focus?

Critical learning points from this chapter

» Technologies don't just mean computers but encompass a wide range of hardware, software, apps and devices that children will encounter in their everyday lives.

» Technologies can be more daunting to adults than to children.

» Children need opportunities to explore different forms of technology associated with the learning of mathematics.

» The mathematical aspects in any technology-related activities need to be made clear and explicit so that connections can be formed between learning in various contexts and using different media.

» It can be difficult to keep up with the rapid changes in technology.

» Technology needs to be used appropriately to support the mathematical concepts being taught and learnt.

Critical reflection

Observe children using different forms of technology and note how often children are engaging with the technology individually and when it is being used as part of the social interactions in the setting. What do you notice about the children's engagement in relation to resilience, concentration and perseverance? How might this be used to plan the next steps for the children's learning of mathematics with the support of technologies?

Observe and listen carefully to children's use of real and pretend technologies in play situations. Again, how might you use this information to assess their skills and plan the next steps in their learning?

Consider creating a play environment with a clear mathematical focus to encourage children to use technologies as part of the play.

Taking it further

Useful books

Aubrey, C and Dahl, S (2008) *A Review of the Evidence on the Use of ICT in the Early Years Foundation Stage*, Research Report. Coventry: British Educational Communications and Technology Agency (BECTA).

> This report looks in detail at differences in attitudes and confidence among practitioners and differences between children in relation to gender.

Roberts-Holmes, G (2013) Playful and Creative ICT Pedagogical Framing: A Nursery School Case Study. *Early Child Development and Care*, 2013: 2–15.

> Although this article doesn't focus specifically on mathematics, it illustrates what is possible with some specialist input at a nursery school.

Useful web-based resources

www.bbc.co.uk/learning/subjects/maths.shtml

> This is an archived BBC webpage with links to mathematics learning resources across the age phases, including a library of video clips from the classroom.

www.bbc.co.uk/schools/websites/4_11/site/numeracy.shtml

> This is a BBC webpage with links to mathematics learning materials suitable for the 4–11 age range.

www.bbc.co.uk/schools/websites/eyfs/

> This BBC website is specific to the Early Years Foundation Stage and points to resources for all areas of learning.

www.crickweb.co.uk/Early-Years.html

> This website provides free access to a wide range of educational resources and games.

nrich.maths.org/frontpage

> NRICH is a Cambridge-based organisation which focuses on working with the more able and gifted children in mathematics. Their website is a good source of open-ended problems (with answers) for the whole education age range. The resources provided on this site are particularly useful if you have identified a young child as being more able in mathematics.

www.ncetm.org.uk

> This is the website of the National Centre for Excellence in the Teaching of Mathematics, covering the whole age range of learners studying mathematics. It has a specific Early Years magazine which contains lots of useful ideas.

www.cimt.plymouth.ac.uk

> This is the website for the Centre for Innovation in Mathematics Teaching. It contains links to learning and teaching resources as well as reports on research projects relating to mathematics education.

www.topmarks.co.uk/Interactive.aspx?cat=1

> This website provides free interactive whiteboard activities.

References

Aubrey, C and Dahl, S (2008) *A Review of the Evidence on the Use of ICT in the Early Years Foundation Stage*, Research Report. Coventry: British Educational Communications and Technology Agency (BECTA).

Flewitt, R (2012) *Multimodal Literacies in the Early Years*. Milton Keynes: Open University.

National Council of Teachers of Mathematics (1998) *Calculators and the Education of Youth*, Position Statement. Reston, Virginia: National Council of Teachers of Mathematics.

National Council of Teachers of Mathematics (2000) *Principles and Standards for School Mathematics*. Reston, Virginia: National Council of Teachers of Mathematics.

Parette, H P, Quesenberry, A C and Blum, C (2010) Missing the Boat with Technology Usage in Early Childhood Settings: A 21st Century View of Developmentally Appropriate Practice. *Early Childhood Education Journal*, 37: 335–43.

Prensky, M (2001) Digital Natives, Digital Immigrants. Part 1. *On the Horizon*, 9(5): 1–6.

Roberts-Holmes, G (2013) Playful and Creative ICT Pedagogical Framing: A Nursery School Case Study. *Early Child Development and Care*, 2013: 2–15.

Shuard, H, Walsh, A, Goodwin, J and Worcester, V (1991) *Calculators, Children and Mathematics*. London: Simon & Schuster.

Somekh, B, Haldane, M, Jones, K, Lewin, C, Steadman, S, Scrimshaw, P, Sing, S, Bird, K, Cummings, J, Downing, B, Harber Stuart, T, Jarvis, J, Mavers, D and Woodrow, D (2007) *Evaluation of the Primary Schools Whiteboard Expansion Project*, Summary Report to the Department for Children, Schools and Families. Manchester Metropolitan University.

10 What happens next?

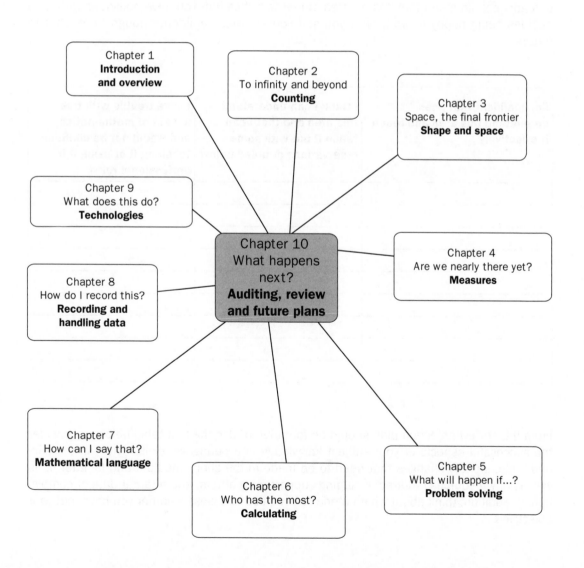

Chapter 1
Introduction and overview

Chapter 2
To infinity and beyond
Counting

Chapter 3
Space, the final frontier
Shape and space

Chapter 9
What does this do?
Technologies

Chapter 10
What happens next?
Auditing, review and future plans

Chapter 4
Are we nearly there yet?
Measures

Chapter 8
How do I record this?
Recording and handling data

Chapter 7
How can I say that?
Mathematical language

Chapter 6
Who has the most?
Calculating

Chapter 5
What will happen if...?
Problem solving

Introduction

This chapter reviews the areas covered in this book and offers some suggestions about how to audit personal subject knowledge and pedagogic skills as well as the mathematics provision in the setting/school. It moves on to show how, using the information obtained from these audits, the practitioner can create a specific action plan for the development of mathematics learning and teaching in the Early Years.

Auditing your own subject knowledge and pedagogic skills

This task is a personal assessment of mathematics subject knowledge, and the reader needs to be honest with themselves regarding how much they know and how confident they feel about various aspects of mathematics. Placing an aspect in the 'I'm confident' category should mean that it is an area of mathematics that you have no issues with, and besides being happy to work on it yourself you are also confident enough to teach it to others.

I'm confident that I can understand this area and teach it effectively	I think I can understand this area and that I can teach it but with some reservations detailed below	I have trouble with this aspect of mathematics and would not be confident teaching it or using it in a professional role

From this review an action plan should be formulated. Use the first table below to consider the successful aspects of your subject knowledge and pedagogic skills. Then, in the second table, identify changes that need to be made in the short, medium and long term, as well as any resources required, including support from others, and a target date of completion. In addition, think about what criteria you will use to assess whether you have met your objectives.

What you are doing well

Action plan for subject knowledge/ pedagogic skills	Areas that need to be improved upon or developed	Resources needed, including support from others	Success criteria	Timescale for completion
Short term				
Medium term				
Long term				

Working on improving subject knowledge and pedagogic skills can take a variety of forms. The most traditional way involves attending a specific course, but you can also consider the following alternatives:

- attending a workshop;
- reading a book;
- reading a research article;
- using internet resources, such as the BBC website Bitesize and mathematical dictionaries;
- watching a video of practice either independently or while discussing it with colleagues;
- watching a colleague at work and then discussing their practice afterwards;
- asking a colleague to watch your practice and discuss it afterwards;
- having a mentor or coach to work with on either subject knowledge or pedagogic skills;
- joining a professional association which focuses on the learning and teaching of mathematics;
- staff meetings;

- informal discussions with colleagues;

- talking to children about preferred models and images they use to support their mathematical thinking;

- visiting other settings/schools to look at different ways of doing things;

- trying different approaches to working with mathematics indoors;

- trying different approaches to working with mathematics outdoors;

- trying an investigation from a web resource such as BEAM or NRICH (see the list of online resources at the end of this chapter);

- working on a piece of mathematics yourself, such as undertaking an investigation or revisiting something you first looked at some time ago;

- offering to test and review new equipment or materials for a manufacturer or publisher;

- journalling your own reflections on practice and subject knowledge.

The main message here is that continuing professional development (CPD) can take any form that is appropriate for you and your circumstances and matches your preferred learning style.

Auditing the provision in your setting/school

In this task, consider the mathematics provision in your setting/school. For each of the aspects of mathematics covered in this book, evaluate the resources and activities available and how they are accessed by the learners.

Aspect of mathematics	Resourcing: Excellent ✓✓✓ Good ✓✓ Fair ✓	Adult-led activities: Frequently ✓✓✓ Occasionally ✓✓ Rarely ✓	Continuous provision: Frequently ✓✓✓ Occasionally ✓✓ Rarely ✓	Play environments: Frequently ✓✓✓ Occasionally ✓✓ Rarely ✓	Indoors ✓✓ Outdoors ✓✓✓
Problem solving					
Mathematical talk					
Counting					
Calculation					
Measures					
Shape and space					
Handling data					
Recording					
Technologies					

After completing this task, the balance of activities and how they are accessed needs to be considered alongside the children's engagement and achievement.

Auditing children's engagement and achievement

This task asks you to look at the engagement and achievement of children in the setting/school. Use this review in conjunction with the review of provision to build up a holistic picture of the mathematics provision in your setting/school and to formulate an action plan.

Aspect of mathematics	Children's engagement: Excellent ✓✓✓ Good ✓✓ Fair ✓	Children's outcomes: Excellent ✓✓✓ Good ✓✓ Fair ✓
Problem solving		
Mathematical talk		
Counting		
Calculation		
Measures		
Shape and space		
Handling data		
Recording		
Technologies		

By looking at the results of this audit alongside the review of provision, you might find that if children do not have access to many activities relating to a particular aspect of mathematics, their engagement and achievement in this area tend to be lower than in areas where they have more access to activities. Children also need a balance of activities to engage successfully with mathematics across the curriculum, which means it is not necessarily beneficial to increase the provision of only adult-led activities, say. The needs of the children come first, and adults should listen to children's preferences in relation to engagement while ensuring that the children have ample opportunities to explore all aspects of mathematics in the setting.

From this review an action plan needs to be formulated. In the first table below, list the successful aspects of the setting/school's provision for learning and teaching. This list can serve as a helpful starting point for discussions or written reports required for an inspection or a more general review of provision. It is also essential to build on successful practice and use the elements of that practice to inform the implementation of any developments. Then, in the second table, identify changes that need to be made in the short, medium and long term, as well as any resources required, including support from others, and a target date of completion. In addition, think about what criteria you will use to assess whether you have met your objectives.

This action plan is structured similarly to the one for personal subject knowledge and pedagogic skills, but this one focuses on the setting/school and is therefore an action plan for a team. Different members of the team can be responsible for collecting information on different aspects of mathematics provision and children's achievement to feed into the review; they could also take a lead on implementing changes in different areas. As a team, plan together how you will work on your CPD; different people in the group are likely to have different learning preferences and, for the action plan to have a greater chance of success, a combination of various approaches will be helpful, so that everyone can feel involved and have their needs met.

What you are doing well

Action plan for the provision for mathematics learning and teaching	Areas that need to be improved upon or developed	Areas that may not have been considered previously	Resources needed, including support and cooperation from others	Lead person	Financial requirements	Success criteria	Timescale for completion
Short term							
Medium term							
Long term							

Critical learning points from this chapter

» Continuing professional development requires a cyclic process of review, action and evaluation.

» Continuing professional development can take a variety of different forms.

» Continuing professional development for teams needs to take account of differences in team members' needs and preferred learning styles.

» Building upon successful practice is essential to the development of learning and teaching of mathematics.

» Children need to have opportunities to explore mathematics in different contexts: adult-led activities, continuous provision and play environments.

»   Children need opportunities to explore mathematics both indoors and outdoors.

»   Adults also need time and support to develop their subject knowledge and pedagogic skills.

Taking it further

Useful books

For further reading, look at any of the articles, books and web resources mentioned at the end of previous chapters in this book.

Useful web-based resources

Kent web: www.kenttrustweb.org.uk/kentict/content/games/maths_menu.html

Coxhoe Primary School: www.schooljotter.com/showpage.php?id=55663

Crickweb: www.crickweb.co.uk/Early-Years.html

Times Educational Supplement: www.tes.co.uk

TES iboard: www.iboard.co.uk

National Centre for Excellence in Teaching Mathematics: www.ncetm.org.uk

Edge Hill University Every Child Counts: everychildcounts.edgehill.ac.uk

Be a Mathematician (BEAM): www.beam.co.uk/mathsofthemonth.php

NRICH: nrich.maths.org

Answers

Chapter 2

Test your subject knowledge (p 20)

1. (a) 9, 19, 29, 39, 49, 59, 69, 79

    (b) 893, 896, 899, 902, 905, 908, 911, 914

    (c) −15, −10, −5, 0, 5, 10, 15

    (d) 8, 28, 48, 68, 88, 108, 128, 148, 168, 188

2. Yes

3. Most people think of π as 22/7 or 3.142, but these are merely abbreviated approximations of the number; the decimal expansion of π goes on for ever and does not contain any repeating pattern, so π is irrational.

Extend your subject knowledge (p 26)

(a) Associative law

(b) Associative law

(c) Commutative law

Chapter 4

Test your subject knowledge (p 65)

1. 5000g

2. 5pm

3. Approximately 100 miles or 160 km

4. Tonnes

5. As a liquid measure, one cup is 250ml. As a dry measure, one cup varies between 110g (eg, butter or cheese) and 350g (eg, golden syrup), depending on what is being measured.

6. Usually half a litre or one litre

Extend your subject knowledge (p 65)

Length	Relationship	Mass/ Weight	Relationship	Capacity	Relationship	Area	Relationship
millimetre (mm)		gram (g)		millilitre (ml)		square millimetre (mm²)	
centimetre (cm)	1cm = 10mm	kilogram (kg)	1 kg = 1000g	centilitre (cl)	1cl = 10ml	square centimetre (cm²)	1cm² = 100mm²
metre (m)	1m = 100cm	tonne	1 tonne = 1000kg	litre (l)	1l = 100cl = 1000ml	square metre (m²)	1m² = 10000cm²
kilometre (km)	1km = 1000m	ounce (oz)	1 ounce = 28.3495g	pint (pt)	1 pint = 0.5683 litres		
inch (in)	1 inch = 2.54cm	pound (lb)	1lb = 16oz	gallon (gal)	1gal = 8pt		
foot (ft)	1ft = 12in						
yard (yd)	1yd = 3ft						
mile (mi)	1mi = 1760yd						

Chapter 5

Test your subject knowledge (p 80)

1. Fifth cross: $5 \times 4 + 1 = 21$; tenth cross: $10 \times 4 + 1 = 41$; nth cross: $4n + 1$
2. There are nine possible team strips ($3 \times 3 \times 3 = 9$).
3. The 35th item in the sequence would have 69 squares; the algebraic expression for the nth item in the sequence is $2n - 1$.

Chapter 6

Test your subject knowledge (p 102)

1. 129
2. 248
3. 899
4. 26
5. 66
6. 91

7. 85

8. 270

9. 522

10. 12

11. 56

13. 97 remainder 3

14. 25.94

Extend your subject knowledge (p 100)

» (a) nine units

(b) one hundred

(c) two thousand

(d) seven hundredths

(e) nine tenths

(f) four thousandths

» (a) 570

(b) 4560

(c) 14

(d) 640

(e) 17

(f) 643

(g) 0.12

(h) 0.032

Glossary

A

Addition — This is the process of joining two or more numbers together to produce a sum or total.

Algorithm — An algorithm is a step-by-step procedure that produces an answer to a particular problem. These are often seen as standard or traditional methods in association with the four rules.

Arithmetic — Arithmetic is a part of mathematics that deals with the properties and handling of number, and their use of counting and calculating. Often seen in the public domain as just covering the four rules – addition, subtraction, multiplication and division.

B

Balance — This is a device for either measuring mass/weight or checking that both sides have the same weight or quantity.

Bar chart — A bar chart or bar graph uses bars to represent quantities against a scale.

C

Calculate — To calculate is to work out or solve a problem or sum.

Calculator — A calculator is a device that performs calculations.

Cardinal — A cardinal number is the total number in a set of objects. It is the final number name that is counted.

Combine — Combining is the process of bringing together two or more quantities in relation to number or measures.

Concept — A set of attributes that defines a unit of knowledge (ie term, class, event, object) and distinguishes it from other units of knowledge.

Counters — Counters can be a set of equipment for sorting and counting. Counters can also be the description of children who can accurately count using the principles of counting.

Counting — Counting is the process of applying a number name to a set of objects in turn to find out how many items there are in the set. It is also the process of reciting a count either in whole numbers 1,2,3,4, or in jumps, 2,4,6,8.

D

Data	This is the information that is collected.
Decimal	This a decimal fraction in the base ten number system shown as a number one or more places to the right of the decimal point.
Decomposition	This is a method of subtraction which breaks down (decomposes) the first number in the operation, where necessary, to allow the subtraction to take place.
Denominator	The bottom number of a fraction is the denominator. This shows how many equal parts something is divided into.
Difference	Difference is the numerical difference between two numbers or it can be seen as subtraction eg the difference between 7 and 3 is 4.
Digits	The digits are the single symbols 0, 1, 2, 3, 4, 5, 6, 7, 8, 9 as used in all numbers.
Dishabituation	This is the reappearance or enhancement of a response to a specific stimulus.
Dividend	This is the number to be divided.
Division	The sharing or grouping of a dividend by the divisor to find the quotient.
Divisor	This the number which will divide the dividend.

E

Even number	A whole number that can be divided equally into two, ie is divisible by 2.

F

Factor	This is a whole number which when multiplied by another results in a product. So 2 x 3 = 6, here 2 and 3 are the factors and 6 is the product. It is also a whole number which divides into another whole number exactly: 12 ÷ 3 = 4, here 3 is a factor of 12, as is 4.
Fraction	A fraction is used to name a part of a group or a whole.

H

Habituation	Habituation is a decrease in response to a stimulus.
Height	This is the vertical measure of length eg from top to bottom.
Histogram	This is a bar graph which represents the frequency distribution for a range of intervals.

I

Iconic	This is a pictorial representation or a sign or graphic symbol whose form suggests meaning.

Idiosyncratic	This is a representation that only has meaning to the person who has created the image.
Irrational number	This is a real number that cannot be written as a fraction. Examples of these are π or $\sqrt{2}$.

K

Known fact	This is an answer to a calculation that is known without having to complete the calculation eg 5 + 5 = 10 or 2 x 5 = 10.

L

Line graph	This is a graph which uses the lines between the data points to represent the information collected.

M

Mean	This is the sum of the data divided by the number of data points, which gives a form of average for the data set.
Measure	This is using a standard unit to find out the quantity or extent or size of items.
Median	This is the middle value of a data set when the data is placed in value order, and this gives a form of average for the data set.
Mode	This is the data point that occurs most often in a set of data.
Multiplication	In its simplest form this is repeated addition.

N

Numeral	A numeral is a digit; it is a symbol used to represent a number.
Numerator	The top number of a fraction is called the numerator. This tells you how many parts you have.
Numerosity	Numerosity is defined by the dictionary as the state of being numerous: numerousness.

O

Odd number	A whole number that is not divisible by 2.
Operation	There are four operations in arithmetic; they are +, −, x and ÷.
Ordinal	This is a number which shows position eg 1st, 2nd, 3rd.

P

Partition	This is about splitting numbers into parts eg 8 can be split into 5 and 3, or partitioning in relation to place value, so 234 is 200, 30 and 4.

Percentage	This is a measure out of 100 eg 20 per cent, 50 per cent.
Pictograms	This is a graph which uses pictures to represent the quantities.
Pictographic	A representation of quantity using pictures but not necessarily pictures of the objects themselves.
Pie chart	This is a graph where data is represented by the division of a circle, where the circle shows the whole population.
Prime	A prime number is a number that only has factors of 1 and itself eg 13.
Problem solving	The process of working out an answer to a problem.
Procept	*An elementary procept is the amalgam of three components: a process which produces a mathematical object, and a symbol which is used to represent either process or object. A procept consists of a collection of elementary procepts which have the same object* (Gray and Tall, 1994).
Product	This is the result (answer) when two numbers are multiplied together.

Q

Quantity	This is the amount or number of an item or group.
Quotient	The result of a division calculation, ie the answer calculated.

R

Range	This is the spread from the lowest value on a graph to the highest value.
Rational number	A rational number can be written as a simple fraction.
Real number	These are positive or negative, decimal or fractional numbers.

S

Statistics	This is the collection, organisation, presentation, interpretation and analysis of data
Subitising	Just seeing how many there are in a group without counting.
Subtract	To take away one quantity from another.
Sum	This can be seen as the total amount. It is also the result of adding two or more quantities together.
Symbol	These are signs to represent actions such as +.
Symbolic	Using symbols to represent quantity.

T

Tally	Marks to represent counting.

Tangram	This is sometimes referred to as a Chinese puzzle. This is a square that is cut into seven pieces. The seven pieces are then arranged into pictures and patterns and the area covered by the pieces remains the same for all images (conservation of area).
Tessellate	When shapes tessellate they fit together without any gaps eg tiling.
Three dimensional (3D)	This is a label given to shapes which have a length, breadth (or width) and height, ie three dimensions.
Total	This is the sum of a set of items, or it can be seen as the result of adding together two or more numbers.
Two dimensional (2D)	This is a label given to plane shapes which have a length and breadth (or width) ie two dimensions.

W

Word problem	This is a calculation problem written in words eg James has two apples and Ellen has three. How many do they have altogether?

Index